Lambert M. Surhone, Miriam T. Timpledon,
Susan F. Marseken (Ed.)

SNAP (software)

Lambert M. Surhone, Miriam T. Timpledon,
Susan F. Marseken (Ed.)

SNAP (software)

Microsoft Windows, Analog Circuits, Linear

Betascript Publishing

Imprint

Permission is granted to copy, distribute and/or modify this document under the terms of the GNU Free Documentation License, Version 1.2 or any later version published by the Free Software Foundation; with no Invariant Sections, with the Front-Cover Texts, and with the Back-Cover Texts. A copy of the license is included in the section entitled "GNU Free Documentation License".

All parts of this book are extracted from Wikipedia, the free encyclopedia (www.wikipedia.org).

You can get detailed informations about the authors of this collection of articles at the end of this book. The editors (Ed.) of this book are no authors. They have not modified or extended the original texts.

Pictures published in this book can be under different licences than the GNU Free Documentation License. You can get detailed informations about the authors and licences of pictures at the end of this book.

The content of this book was generated collaboratively by volunteers. Please be advised that nothing found here has necessarily been reviewed by people with the expertise required to provide you with complete, accurate or reliable information. Some information in this book maybe misleading or wrong. The Publisher does not guarantee the validity of the information found here. If you need specific advice (f.e. in fields of medical, legal, financial, or risk management questions) please contact a professional who is licensed or knowledgeable in that area.

Any brand names and product names mentioned in this book are subject to trademark, brand or patent protection and are trademarks or registered trademarks of their respective holders. The use of brand names, product names, common names, trade names, product descriptions etc. even without a particular marking in this works is in no way to be construed to mean that such names may be regarded as unrestricted in respect of trademark and brand protection legislation and could thus be used by anyone.

Cover image: www.ingimage.com
Concerning the licence of the cover image please contact ingimage.

Contact:
VDM Publishing House Ltd.,17 Rue Meldrum, Beau Bassin,1713-01 Mauritius
Email: info@vdm-publishing-house.com
Website: www.vdm-publishing-house.com

Published in 2010
Printed in: U.S.A., U.K., Germany. This book was not produced in Mauritius.

ISBN: 978-613-2-10750-3

Contents

Articles

Articles

References

Article Licenses

SNAP (software)

SNAP (Symbolic Network Analysis Program) is a symbolic circuit simulator for the Windows environment. Unlike more common numerical circuit simulators (such as SPICE), SNAP can generate analytical Laplace domain expressions for arbitrary network functions of linear analog circuits. The SNAP package also includes tools for schematic capture and graphic post-processing as well as advanced features such as Parameter Stepping, a Dependences Editor and the ability to export results to various, analysis software.

SNAP is available for free from its homepage.

See also

- SapWin
- Symbolic Circuit Analysis

External links

- Snap Survey Software [1]
- SNAP homepage [2]

Microsoft Windows

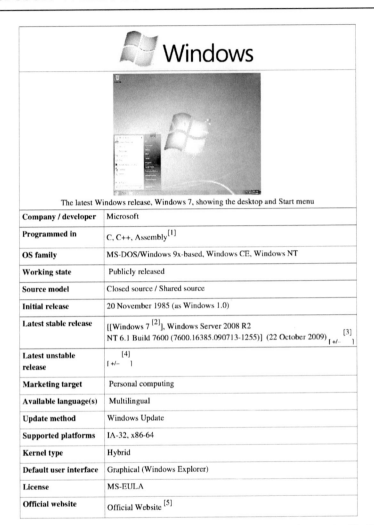

The latest Windows release, Windows 7, showing the desktop and Start menu

Company / developer	Microsoft
Programmed in	C, C++, Assembly[1]
OS family	MS-DOS/Windows 9x-based, Windows CE, Windows NT
Working state	Publicly released
Source model	Closed source / Shared source
Initial release	20 November 1985 (as Windows 1.0)
Latest stable release	[[Windows 7 [2]], Windows Server 2008 R2 NT 6.1 Build 7600 (7600.16385.090713-1255)] (22 October 2009) [3] [+/-]
Latest unstable release	[4] [+/-]
Marketing target	Personal computing
Available language(s)	Multilingual
Update method	Windows Update
Supported platforms	IA-32, x86-64
Kernel type	Hybrid
Default user interface	Graphical (Windows Explorer)
License	MS-EULA
Official website	Official Website [5]

Microsoft Windows is a series of software operating systems and graphical user interfaces produced by Microsoft. Microsoft first introduced an operating environment named *Windows* in November 1985 as an add-on to MS-DOS in response to the growing interest in graphical user interfaces (GUIs).[2] Microsoft Windows came to dominate the world's personal computer market, overtaking Mac OS, which had been introduced previously. As of October 2009, Windows had approximately 91% of the market share of the client operating systems for usage on the Internet.[3] [4] [5] The most recent client version of Windows is Windows 7; the most recent server version is Windows Server 2008 R2; the most recent mobile OS version is Windows Mobile 6.5.

Versions

The term *Windows* collectively describes any or all of several generations of Microsoft operating system products. These products are generally categorized as follows:

Early versions

Windows 1.0, the first version, released in 1985

The history of Windows dates back to September 1981, when the project named "Interface Manager" was started. It was announced in November 1983 (after the Apple Lisa, but before the Macintosh) under the name "Windows", but Windows 1.0 was not released until November 1985.[6] The shell of Windows 1.0 was a program known as the MS-DOS Executive. Other supplied programs were Calculator, Calendar, Cardfile, Clipboard viewer, Clock, Control Panel, Notepad, Paint, Reversi, Terminal, and Write. Windows 1.0 did not allow overlapping windows, due to Apple Computer owning this feature. Instead all windows were tiled. Only dialog boxes could appear over other windows.

Windows 2.0 was released in October 1987 and featured several improvements to the user interface and memory management.[6] Windows 2.0 allowed application windows to overlap each other and also introduced more sophisticated keyboard-shortcuts. It could also make use of expanded memory.

Windows 2.1 was released in two different flavors: Windows/386 employed the 386 virtual 8086 mode to multitask several DOS programs, and the paged memory model to emulate expanded memory using available extended memory. Windows/286 (which, despite its name, would run on the 8086) still ran in real mode, but could make use of the high memory area.

The early versions of Windows were often thought of as simply graphical user interfaces, mostly because they ran on top of MS-DOS and used it for file system services.[7] However, even the earliest 16-bit Windows versions already assumed many typical operating system functions; notably, having their own executable file format and providing their own device drivers (timer, graphics, printer, mouse, keyboard and sound) for applications. Unlike MS-DOS, Windows allowed users to execute multiple graphical applications at the same time, through cooperative multitasking. Windows implemented an elaborate, segment-based, software virtual memory scheme, which allowed it to run applications larger than available memory: code segments and resources were swapped in and thrown away when memory became scarce, and data segments moved in memory when a given application had relinquished processor control, typically waiting for user input.

Windows OS market share

Source	Net Market Share[8]	W3Counter[9]	StatCounter[10]
Date	*May 2010*	*May 2010*	*May 2010*
All versions	91.16%	83.11%	92.32%
Windows XP	62.55%	49.95%	58.02%
Windows Vista	15.25%	17.6%	19.46%
Windows 7	12.68%	14.33%	14.84%
Windows 2000	0.5%	0.34%	—
Windows 98	0.1%	—	—
Windows Me	0.08%	—	—

Windows Server 2003	—	0.89%	—

Windows 3.0 and 3.1

Windows 3.0 (1990) and Windows 3.1 (1992) improved the design, mostly because of virtual memory and loadable virtual device drivers (VxDs) which allowed them to share arbitrary devices between multitasked DOS windows. Also, Windows applications could now run in protected mode (when Windows was running in Standard or 386 Enhanced Mode), which gave them access to several megabytes of memory and removed the obligation to participate in the software virtual memory scheme. They still ran inside the same address space, where the segmented memory provided a degree of protection, and multi-tasked cooperatively. For Windows 3.0, Microsoft also rewrote critical operations from C into assembly, making this release faster and

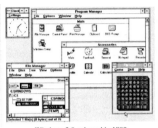

Windows 3.0, released in 1990

less memory-hungry than its predecessors. With the introduction of Windows for Workgroups 3.11, Windows was able to bypass DOS for file management operations using 32-bit file access.

Windows 95, 98, and Me

Windows 95 was released in August 1995, featuring a new user interface, support for long file names of up to 255 characters, and the ability to automatically detect and configure installed hardware (plug and play). It could natively run 32-bit applications, and featured several technological improvements that increased its stability over Windows 3.1. There were several OEM Service Releases (OSR) of Windows 95, each of which was roughly equivalent to a service pack.

Microsoft's next release was Windows 98 in June 1998. Microsoft released a second version of Windows 98 in May 1999, named Windows 98 Second Edition (often shortened to Windows 98 SE).

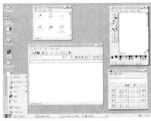

Windows 95, released in 1995

In September 2000, Microsoft released Windows Me (*Me* standing for *Millennium Edition*), which updated the core from Windows 98 but adopted some aspects of Windows 2000 and removed the "boot in DOS mode" option. It also added a new feature called System Restore, allowing the user to set the computer's settings back to an earlier date.

Windows NT family

The NT family of Windows systems was fashioned and marketed for higher reliability business use. The first release was NT 3.1 (1993), numbered "3.1" to match the consumer Windows version, which was followed by NT 3.5 (1994), NT 3.51 (1995), NT 4.0 (1996), and Windows 2000 (2000). 2000 is the last NT-based Windows release which does not include Microsoft Product Activation. NT 4.0 was the first in this line to implement the "Windows 95" user interface (and the first to include Windows 95's built-in 32-bit runtimes).

Microsoft then moved to combine their consumer and business operating systems with Windows XP, coming in both home and professional versions (and later niche market versions for tablet PCs and media centers); they also diverged release schedules for server operating systems. Windows Server 2003, released a year and a half after Windows XP, brought Windows Server up to date with MS Windows XP. After a lengthy development process, Windows Vista was released toward the end of 2006, and its server counterpart, Windows Server 2008 was released in early 2008. On July 22, 2009, Windows 7 and Windows Server 2008 R2 were released as RTM (release to manufacturing). Windows 7 was released on October 22, 2009.

64-bit operating systems

Windows NT included support for several different platforms before the x86-based personal computer became dominant in the professional world. Versions of NT from 3.1 to 4.0 variously supported PowerPC, DEC Alpha and MIPS R4000, some of which were 64-bit processors, although the operating system treated them as 32-bit processors.

With the introduction of the Intel Itanium architecture (also known as IA-64), Microsoft released new versions of Windows to support it. Itanium versions of Windows XP and Windows Server 2003 were released at the same time as their mainstream x86 (32-bit) counterparts. On April 25, 2005, Microsoft released Windows XP Professional x64 Edition and Windows Server 2003 x64 Editions to support the x86-64 (or *x64* in Microsoft terminology) architecture. Microsoft dropped support for the Itanium version of Windows XP in 2005. Windows Vista is the first end-user version of Windows that Microsoft has released simultaneously in x86 and x64 editions. Windows Vista does not support the Itanium architecture. The modern 64-bit Windows family comprises AMD64/Intel64 versions of Windows Vista, and Windows Server 2008, in both Itanium and x64 editions. Windows Server 2008 R2 drops the 32-bit version, although Windows 7 does not.

Windows CE

Windows CE (officially known as *Windows Embedded Compact*), is an edition of Windows that runs on minimalistic computers, like satellite navigation systems and some mobile phones. Windows Embedded Compact is based on its own dedicated kernel, dubbed Windows CE kernel. Microsoft licenses Windows CE to OEMs and device makers. The OEMs and device makers can modify and create their own user interfaces and experiences, while Windows CE provides the technical foundation to do so.

The latest upcoming version of Windows CE, Windows Embedded Compact 7, displaying a possible UI for what the media player can look like.

Windows CE was used in the Dreamcast along with Sega's own proprietary OS for the console. Windows CE is the core from which Windows Mobile is derived. Microsoft's latest upcoming version of their mobile OS, Windows Phone 7, is based on components from both Windows CE 6.0 R3 and the upcoming Windows CE 7.0.

Windows Embedded Compact is not to be confused with Windows XP Embedded or Windows NT 4.0 Embedded, modular editions of Windows based on Windows NT kernel.

Future

Windows 8, the successor to Windows 7, is currently in development.

History

The Windows family tree.

Microsoft has taken two parallel routes in its operating systems. One route has been for the home user and the other has been for the professional IT user. The dual routes have generally led to home versions having greater multimedia support and less functionality in networking and security, and professional versions having inferior multimedia support and better networking and security.

The first version of Microsoft Windows, version 1.0, released in November 1985, lacked a degree of functionality and achieved little popularity, and was to compete with Apple's own operating system. Windows 1.0 is not a complete operating system; rather, it extends MS-DOS. Microsoft Windows version 2.0 was released in November, 1987 and was slightly more popular than its predecessor. Windows 2.03 (release date January 1988) had changed the OS from tiled windows to overlapping windows. The result of this change led to Apple Computer filing a suit against Microsoft alleging infringement on Apple's copyrights.[11] [12]

Microsoft Windows 3.0, released in 1990, was the first Microsoft Windows version to achieve broad commercial success, selling 2 million copies in the first six months.[13] [14] It featured improvements to the user interface and to multitasking capabilities. It received a facelift in Windows 3.1, made generally available on March 1, 1992. Windows 3.1 support ended on December 31, 2001.[15]

In July 1993, Microsoft released Windows NT based on a new kernel. NT was considered to be the professional OS and was the first Windows version to utilize preemptive multitasking.. Windows NT would later be retooled to also function as a home operating system, with Windows XP.

On August 24, 1995, Microsoft released Windows 95, a new, and major, consumer version that made further changes to the user interface, and also used preemptive multitasking. Windows 95 was designed to replace not only Windows 3.1, but also Windows for Workgroups, and MS-DOS. It was also the first Windows operating system to use Plug and Play capabilities. The changes Windows 95 brought to the desktop were revolutionary, as opposed to evolutionary, such as those in Windows 98 and Windows Me. Mainstream support for Windows 95 ended on December 31, 2000 and extended support for Windows 95 ended on December 31, 2001.[16]

The next in the consumer line was Microsoft Windows 98 released on June 25, 1998. It was substantially criticized for its slowness and for its unreliability compared with Windows 95, but many of its basic problems were later rectified with the release of Windows 98 Second Edition (98SE) in 1999. Mainstream support for Windows 98 ended on June 30, 2002 and extended support for Windows 98 ended on July 11, 2006.[17]

As part of its "professional" line, Microsoft released Windows 2000 in February 2000. During 2004 part of the Source Code for Windows 2000 was leaked onto the internet. This was bad for Microsoft as the same kernel used in Windows 2000 was used in Windows XP. The consumer version following Windows 98 was Windows Me (Windows Millennium Edition). Released in September 2000, Windows Me implemented a number of new technologies for Microsoft: most notably publicized was "Universal Plug and Play". Windows Me was criticized a lot, due to slownesses, freezes and hardware problems.

In October 2001, Microsoft released Windows XP, a version built on the Windows NT kernel that also retained the consumer-oriented usability of Windows 95 and its successors. This new version was widely praised in computer magazines.[18] It shipped in two distinct editions, "Home" and "Professional", the former lacking many of the superior security and networking features of the Professional edition. Additionally, the first "Media Center" edition was released in 2002,[19] with an emphasis on support for DVD and TV functionality including program recording and a remote control. Mainstream support for Windows XP ended on April 14, 2009. Extended support will continue until April 8, 2014.[20]

In April 2003, Windows Server 2003 was introduced, replacing the Windows 2000 line of server products with a number of new features and a strong focus on security; this was followed in December 2005 by Windows Server 2003 R2.

On January 30, 2007 Microsoft released Windows Vista. It contains a number of new features, from a redesigned shell and user interface to significant technical changes, with a particular focus on security features. It is available in a number of different editions, and has been subject to some criticism.

Timeline of releases

Timeline of releases				
Release date	Product name	Current Version / Build	Notes	Last IE
November 1985	Windows 1.01	1.01	Unsupported	-
November 1987	Windows 2.03	2.03	Unsupported	-
May 1988	Windows 2.10	2.10	Unsupported	-
March 1989	Windows 2.11	2.11	Unsupported	-
May 1990	Windows 3.0	3.0	Unsupported	-
March 1992	Windows 3.1x	3.1	Unsupported	5
October 1992	Windows For Workgroups 3.1	3.1	Unsupported	5
July 1993	Windows NT 3.1	NT 3.1	Unsupported	5
December 1993	Windows For Workgroups 3.11	3.11	Unsupported	5
January 1994	Windows 3.2 (released in Simplified Chinese only)	3.2	Unsupported	5
September 1994	Windows NT 3.5	NT 3.5	Unsupported	5
May 1995	Windows NT 3.51	NT 3.51	Unsupported	5
August 1995	Windows 95	4.0.950	Unsupported	5.5
July 1996	Windows NT 4.0	NT 4.0.1381	Unsupported	6
June 1998	Windows 98	4.10.1998	Unsupported	6
May 1999	Windows 98 SE	4.10.2222	Unsupported	6
February 2000	Windows 2000	NT 5.0.2195	Extended Support until July 13, 2010[21]	6
September 2000	Windows Me	4.90.3000	Unsupported	6
October 2001	Windows XP	NT 5.1.2600	Extended Support until July 13, 2010 for SP2 and April 8, 2014 for SP3. (RTM and SP1 unsupported).	8

March 2003	Windows XP 64-bit Edition (IA-64)	NT 5.2.3790	Unsupported	6
April 2003	Windows Server 2003	NT 5.2.3790	Current (RTM unsupported).	8
April 2005	Windows XP Professional x64 Edition	NT 5.2.3790	Extended Support until July 13, 2010 for SP2 and April 8, 2014 for SP3. (RTM and SP1 unsupported).	8
July 2006	Windows Fundamentals for Legacy PCs	NT 5.1.2600	Current	8
November 2006 (volume licensing) January 2007 (retail)	Windows Vista	NT 6.0.6002	Current (RTM unsupported). Version changed to NT 6.0.6001 with SP1 (February 4, 2008) and to NT 6.0.6002 with SP2 (April 28, 2009).	9
July 2007	Windows Home Server	NT 5.2.4500	Current	8
February 2008	Windows Server 2008	NT 6.0.6002	Current Version changed to NT 6.0.6002 with SP2 (April 28, 2009).	9
October 2009 [22]	Windows 7 and Windows Server 2008 R2	NT 6.1.7600	Current	9
2012	Windows 8	Unknown	Upcoming	Unknown

Security

Consumer versions of Windows were originally designed for ease-of-use on a single-user PC without a network connection, and did not have security features built in from the outset.[23] However, Windows NT and its successors are designed for security (including on a network) and multi-user PCs, but were not initially designed with Internet security in mind as much, since, when it was first developed in the early 1990s, Internet use was less prevalent.[24]

These design issues combined with programming errors (e.g. buffer overflows) and the popularity of Windows means that it is a frequent target of computer worm and virus writers. In June 2005, Bruce Schneier's *Counterpane Internet Security* reported that it had seen over 1,000 new viruses and worms in the previous six months.[25]

Microsoft releases security patches through its Windows Update service approximately once a month (usually the second Tuesday of the month), although critical updates are made available at shorter intervals when necessary.[26] In versions of Windows after and including Windows 2000 SP3 and Windows XP, updates can be automatically downloaded and installed if the user selects to do so. As a result, Service Pack 2 for Windows XP, as well as Service Pack 1 for Windows Server 2003, were installed by users more quickly than it otherwise might have been.[27]

While the Windows 9x series offered the option of having profiles for multiple users, they had no concept of access privileges, and did not allow concurrent access; and so were not true multi-user operating systems. In addition, they implemented only partial memory protection. They were accordingly widely criticised for lack of security.

The Windows NT series of operating systems, by contrast, are true multi-user, and implement absolute memory protection. However, a lot of the advantages of being a true multi-user operating system were nullified by the fact that, prior to Windows Vista, the first user account created during the setup process was an administrator account, which was also the default for new accounts. Though Windows XP did have limited accounts, the majority of home users did not change to an account type with fewer rights – partially due to the number of programs which unnecessarily required administrator rights – and so most home users ran as administrator all the time.

Windows Vista changes this[28] by introducing a privilege elevation system called User Account Control. When logging in as a standard user, a logon session is created and a token containing only the most basic privileges is assigned. In this way, the new logon session is incapable of making changes that would affect the entire system. When logging in as a user in the Administrators group, two separate tokens are assigned. The first token contains all privileges typically awarded to an administrator, and the second is a restricted token similar to what a standard user would receive. User applications, including the Windows Shell, are then started with the restricted token, resulting in a reduced privilege environment even under an Administrator account. When an application requests higher privileges or "Run as administrator" is clicked, UAC will prompt for confirmation and, if consent is given (including administrator credentials if the account requesting the elevation is not a member of the administrators group), start the process using the unrestricted token.[29]

File permissions

All Windows versions from Windows NT 3 have been based on a file system permission system referred to as AGLP (Accounts, Global, Local, Permissions) AGDLP which in essence where file permissions are applied to the file/folder in the form of a 'local group' which then has other 'global groups' as members. These global groups then hold other groups or users depending on different Windows versions used. This system varies from other vendor products such as Linux and NetWare due to the 'static' allocation of permission being applied directory to the file or folder. However using this process of AGLP/AGDLP/AGUDLP allows a small number of static permissions to be applied and allows for easy changes to the account groups without reapplying the file permissions on the files and folders.

Windows Defender

On January 6, 2005, Microsoft released a Beta version of Microsoft AntiSpyware, based upon the previously released Giant AntiSpyware. On February 14, 2006, Microsoft AntiSpyware became Windows Defender with the release of Beta 2. Windows Defender is a freeware program designed to protect against spyware and other unwanted software. Windows XP and Windows Server 2003 users who have genuine copies of Microsoft Windows can freely download the program from Microsoft's web site, and Windows Defender ships as part of Windows Vista and 7.[30]

Third-party analysis

In an article based on a report by Symantec,[31] internetnews.com has described Microsoft Windows as having the "fewest number of patches and the shortest average patch development time of the five operating systems it monitored in the last six months of 2006."[32]

A study conducted by Kevin Mitnick and marketing communications firm Avantgarde in 2004 found that an unprotected and unpatched Windows XP system with Service Pack 1 lasted only 4 minutes on the Internet before it was compromised, and an unprotected and also unpatched Windows Server 2003 system was compromised after being connected to the internet for 8 hours.[33] However, it is important to note that this study does not apply to Windows XP systems running the Service Pack 2 update (released in late 2004), which vastly improved the security of Windows XP. The computer that was running Windows XP Service Pack 2 was not compromised. The AOL National Cyber Security Alliance Online Safety Study of October 2004 determined that 80% of Windows users were infected by at least one spyware/adware product.[34] Much documentation is available describing how to increase the security of Microsoft Windows products. Typical suggestions include deploying Microsoft Windows behind a hardware or software firewall, running anti-virus and anti-spyware software, and installing patches as they become available through Windows Update.[35]

Emulation software

Emulation allows the use of some Windows applications without using Microsoft Windows. These include:

- Wine — a free and open source software implementation of the Windows API, allowing one to run many Windows applications on x86-based platforms, including Linux and Mac OS X. Wine developers refer to it as a "compatibility layer";[36] and make use of Windows-style APIs to emulate the Windows environment.
  - CrossOver — A Wine package with licensed fonts. Its developers are regular contributors to Wine, and focus on Wine running officially supported applications.
  - Cedega — TransGaming Technologies' proprietary fork of Wine, designed specifically for running games written for Microsoft Windows under Linux. A version of Cedega known as Cider is used by some video game publishers to allow Windows games to run on Mac OS X. Since wine was licensed under the LGPL Cedega has been unable to port the improvements made to wine to their proprietary codebase.
  - Darwine — A bundling of Wine to the PowerPC Macs running OS X by running wine on top of QEMU. Intel Macs use the same Wine as other *NIX x86 systems.
- ReactOS — An open-source OS that is intended to run the same software as Windows, originally designed to simulate Windows NT 4.0, now aiming at Windows XP compatibility. It has been in the development stage since 1996.

See also

General:

- Comparison of operating systems
- Comparison of Windows and Linux
- Comparison of Windows versions
- List of operating systems
- Market share of operating systems

Further reading:

- Microsoft Security Essentials
- Architecture of the Windows NT operating system line
- Criticism of Microsoft Windows
- List of Microsoft Windows components
- Microsoft Windows topics
- Optimization (Infrastructure & Application Platform)
- Windows Explorer
- Windows Genuine Advantage
- Windows Media
- Windows Startup Process
- Wintel

External links

- Official Microsoft Windows Website [41]
- Microsoft Developer Network [42]
- Microsoft Windows History Timeline [43]
- Pearson Education, InformIT [44] – History of Microsoft Windows

References

[1] Microsoft Windows System Overview (http://www.microsoft.com/technet/archive/winntas/training/ntarchitectoview/ntarc_2.mspx)

[2] "The Unusual History of Microsoft Windows" (http://inventors.about.com/od/mstartinventions/a/Windows.htm?rd=1). . Retrieved 2007-04-22.

[3] "Global Web Stats" (http://www.w3counter.com/globalstats.php). W3Counter, Awio Web Services. September 2009. . Retrieved 2009-10-24.

[4] "Operating System Market Share" (http://marketshare.hitslink.com/operating-system-market-share.aspx?qprid=8). Net Applications. October 2009. . Retrieved November 5, 2009.

[5] "Top 5 Operating Systems on Oct 09" (http://gs.statcounter.com/#os-ww-monthly-200910-200910-bar). StatCounter. October 2009. . Retrieved November 5, 2009.

[6] Petzold

[7] "Windows Evolution" (http://news.soft32.com/windows-evolution_1629.html). Soft32.com News. .

[8] "Net Applications Operating System Market Share" (http://marketshare.hitslink.com/operating-system-market-share.aspx?qprid=10&qpcal=1&qpcal=1&qpcal=1&qptimeframe=M&qpsp=136). Net Market Share. May 2010. .

[9] "Global Web Stats" (http://w3counter.com/globalstats.php?year=2010&month=5). W3Counter. May 2010. .

[10] "StatCounter Global Stats" (http://gs.statcounter.com/#os-ww-monthly-201005-201005-bar). StatCounter. May 2010. .

[11] "The Apple vs. Microsoft GUI Lawsuit" (http://lowendmac.com/orchard/06/apple-vs-microsoft.html). 2006. . Retrieved 2008-03-12

[12] "Apple Computer, Inc. v. MicroSoft Corp., 35 F.3d 1435 (9th Cir. 1994)" (http://home.earthlink.net/~mjohnsen/Technology/Lawsuits/appvsms.html). . Retrieved 2008-03-12

[13] "Chronology of Personal Computer Software" (http://www.islandnet.com/~kpolsson/compsoft/soft1991.htm). .

[14] "Microsoft Company" (http://www.thocp.net/companies/microsoft/microsoft_company.htm). .

[15] Windows 3.1 Standard Edition Support Lifecycle (http://support.microsoft.com/lifecycle/?p1=3078)

[16] Windows 95 Support Lifecycle (http://support.microsoft.com/lifecycle/?p1=7864)

[17] Windows 98 Standard Edition Support Lifecycle (http://support.microsoft.com/lifecycle/?p1=6513)

[18] Your top Windows XP questions answered! (Part One) (http://web.archive.org/web/20071219121319/http://review.zdnet.com/4520-6033_16-4206367.html)

[19] Paul Thurrott's SuperSite for Windows: A Look at Freestyle and Mira (http://www.winsupersite.com/showcase/freestyle_preview.asp)

[20] Windows XP Professional Lifecycle Support (http://support.microsoft.com/lifecycle/?p1=3223)

[21] "Windows 2000 Professional Edition Support Lifecycle" (http://support.microsoft.com/lifecycle/?p1=3071). Microsoft. May 4, 2005. . Retrieved 2007-03-25.

[22] "Microsoft Delivers New Wave of Technologies to Help Businesses Thrive in Today's Economy" (http://www.microsoft.com/presspass/press/2009/May09/05-11TechEd09PR.mspx?rss_fdn=Press Releases). Microsoft. 2009-05-11. . Retrieved 2009-05-22.

[23] Multi-user memory protection was not introduced until Windows NT and XP, and a computer's default user was an administrator until Windows Vista. Source: UAC msdn (http://blogs.msdn.com/uac/)

[24] "Telephones and Internet Users by Country, 1990 and 2005" (http://www.infoplease.com/ipa/A0883396.html). Information Please Database. . Retrieved 2009-06-09.

[25] Schneier, Bruce (2005-06-15). "Crypto-Gram Newsletter" (http://www.schneier.com/crypto-gram-0506.html). Counterpane Internet Security, Inc.. . Retrieved 2007-04-22.

[26] Naraine, Ryan (2005-06-08). "Microsoft's Security Response Center: How Little Patches Are Made" (http://www.eweek.com/c/a/Windows/Microsofts-Security-Response-Center-How-Little-Patches-Are-Made/). eWeek. . Retrieved 2007-04-22.

[27] Foley, John (2004-10-20). "Windows XP SP2 Distribution Surpasses 100 Million" (http://www.informationweek.com/news/security/vulnerabilities/showArticle.jhtml?articleID=50900297). InformationWeek. . Retrieved 2007-04-22.

[28] Microsoft describes in detail the steps taken to combat this in a TechNet bulletin. (http://technet.microsoft.com/en-us/windowsvista/aa905073.aspx)

[29] Kenny Kerr (2006-09-29). "Windows Vista for Developers – Part 4 – User Account Control" (http://weblogs.asp.net/kennykerr/archive/2006/09/29/Windows-Vista-for-Developers-_1320_-Part-4-_1320_-User-Account-Control.aspx). . Retrieved 2007-03-15.

[30] "Windows Vista: Features" (http://www.Microsoft.com/Windowsvista/features/foreveryone/security.mspx). MicroSoft. . Retrieved 2006-07-20.

[31] "Symantec 11th Internet Security Threat Report, Trends for July–December 6" (http://www.symantec.com/business/theme.jsp?themeid=threatreport). .

[32] "Report Says Windows Gets The Fastest Repairs" (http://www.internetnews.com/security/article.php/3667201). .
[33] "Automated "Bots" Overtake PCs Without Firewalls Within 4 Minutes" (http://www.avantgarde.com/ttln113004.html). Avant Garde. .
[34] "Safety Study" (http://web.archive.org/web/20051102045804/http://www.staysafeonline.info/pdf/safety_study_v04.pdf) (PDF).
   Stay Safe Online. Archived from the original (http://www.staysafeonline.info/pdf/safety_study_v04.pdf) on 2005-11-02. .
[35] 5 Steps to Securing Your Windows XP Home Computer (http://www.computer-security-news.com/0969/
   5-steps-to-securing-your-windows-xp-home-computer)
[36] "Wine" (http://www.winehq.org/). .

Analog circuits

Analogue electronics (or **analog** in American English) are electronic systems with a continuously variable signal, in contrast to digital electronics where signals usually take only two different levels. The term "analogue" describes the proportional relationship between a signal and a voltage or current that represents the signal. The word analogue is derived from the Greek word ανάλογος (analogos) meaning "proportional".[1]

Analogue signals

An analogue signal uses some attribute of the medium to convey the signal's information. For example, an aneroid barometer uses the angular position of a needle as the signal to convey the information of changes in atmospheric pressure.[2] Electrical signals may represent information by changing their voltage, current, frequency, or total charge. Information is converted from some other physical form (such as sound, light, temperature, pressure, position) to an electrical signal by a transducer which converts one type of energy into another e. g. a microphone.[3]

The signals take any value from a given range, and each unique signal value represents different information. Any change in the signal is meaningful, and each level of the signal represents a different level of the phenomenon that it represents. For example, suppose the signal is being used to represent temperature, with one volt representing one degree Celsius. In such a system 10 volts would represent 10 degrees, and 10.1 volts would represent 10.1 degrees.

Another method of conveying an analogue signal is to use modulation. In this, some base carrier signal has one of its properties altered: amplitude modulation (AM) involves altering the amplitude of a sinusoidal voltage waveform by the source information, frequency modulation (FM) changes the frequency. Other techniques, such as phase modulation or changing the phase of the carrier signal, are also used.[4]

In an analogue sound recording, the variation in pressure of a sound striking a microphone creates a corresponding variation in the current passing through it or voltage across it. An increase in the volume of the sound causes the fluctuation of the current or voltage to increase proportionally while keeping the same waveform or shape.

Mechanical, pneumatic, hydraulic and other systems may also use analogue signals.

Inherent noise

Analogue systems invariably include noise; that is, random disturbances or variations, some caused by the random thermal vibrations of atomic particles. Since all variations of an analogue signal are significant, any disturbance is equivalent to a change in the original signal and so appears as noise.[5] As the signal is copied and re-copied, or transmitted over long distances, these random variations become more significant and lead to signal degradation. Other sources of noise may include external electrical signals or poorly designed components. These disturbances are reduced by shielding, and using low-noise amplifiers (LNA).[6]

Analogue vs. digital electronics

Since the information is encoded differently in analogue and digital electronics, the way they process a signal is consequently different. All operations that can be performed on an analogue signal such as amplification, filtering, limiting, and others, can also be duplicated in the digital domain. Every digital circuit is also an analogue circuit, in that the behaviour of any digital circuit can be explained using the rules of analogue circuits.

The first electronic devices invented and mass produced were analogue. The use of microelectronics has reduced the cost of digital techniques and now make digital methods feasible and cost-effective such as in the field of human-machine communication by voice.[7]

The main differences between analogue and digital electronics are listed below:

Noise

Because of the way information is encoded in analogue circuits, they are much more susceptible to noise than digital circuits, since a small change in the signal can represent a significant change in the information present in the signal and can cause the information present to be lost. Since digital signals take on one of only two different values, a disturbance would have to be about one-half the magnitude of the digital signal to cause an error; this property of digital circuits can be exploited to make signal processing noise-resistant. In digital electronics, because the information is quantized, as long as the signal stays inside a range of values, it represents the same information. Digital circuits use this principle to regenerate the signal at each logic gate, lessening or removing noise.[8]

Precision

A number of factors affect how precise a signal is, mainly the noise present in the original signal and the noise added by processing. See signal-to-noise ratio. Fundamental physical limits such as the shot noise in components limits the resolution of analogue signals. In digital electronics additional precision is obtained by using additional digits to represent the signal; the practical limit in the number of digits is determined by the performance of the analogue-to-digital converter(ADC), since digital operations can usually be performed without loss of precision. The ADC takes an analogue signal and changes into a series of binary numbers. The ADC may be used in simple digital display devices e. g. thermometers, light meters but it may also be used in digital sound recording and in data acquisition. However, a digital-to-analogue converter(DAC) is used to change a digital signal to an analogue signal. A DAC takes a series of binary numbers and converts it to an analogue signal. It is common to find a DAC in the gain-control system of an op-amp which in turn may be used to control digital amplifiers and filters.[9]

Design difficulty

Analogue circuits are harder to design, requiring more skill, than comparable digital systems. This is one of the main reasons why digital systems have become more common than analogue devices. An analogue circuit must be designed by hand, and the process is much less automated than for digital systems. However, if a digital electronic device is to interact with the real world, it will always need an analogue interface.[10] For example, every digital radio receiver has an analogue preamplifier as the first stage in the receive chain.

See also

- Analogue computer
- Analogue signal
- Digital - See here for a discussion of digital vs. analogue.
- Analogue recording vs. digital recording
- Analogue chip
- Analogue verification

External links

- Analog Design center [11]

References

[1] *Concise Oxford dictionary* (10 ed.). Oxford University Press Inc.. 1999. ISBN 0198602871.

[2] Plympton, George Washington (1884). *The aneroid barometer: its construction and use* (http://books.google.com/ books?id=rzM7AAAAMAAJ&printsec=frontcover&dq=aneroid+barometer#v=onepage&q=&f=false). D. Van Nostran Co.. .

[3] Singmin, Andrew (2001). *Beginning digital electronics through projects* (http://books.google.com/books?id=av_37zMG5H4C& pg=PA9&dq=analogue+electronics+transducer#v=onepage&q=&f=false). Newnes. p. 9. ISBN 0750672696. . "Signals come from transducers..."

[4] Miller, Mark R. (2002). *Electronics the Easy Way* (http://books.google.com/books?id=FEdLZZgCe6YC&pg=PA232&dq=Electronics+ the+easy+way+modulation+&+demodulation#v=onepage&q=&f=false). Barron's Educational Series. pp. 232–239. ISBN 0764119811. . "Until the radio came along..."

[5] Hsu, Hwei Piao (2003). *Schaum's outline of theory and problems of analogue and digital communications* (http://books.google.com/ books?id=02I-J_ZQa50C&pg=PA202&dq=analogue+system+noise#v=onepage&q=&f=false). McGraw-Hill Professional. p. 202. ISBN 0071402286. . "The presence of noise degrades the performance of communication systems."

[6] Carr, Joseph J. (2000). *Secrets of RF circuit design* (http://books.google.com/books?id=begI88-yUBwC&pg=PA423&dq=low+noise+ amplifiers#v=onepage&q=low noise amplifiers&f=false). McGraw-Hill Professional. p. 423. ISBN 0071370677. . "It is common in microwave systems..."

[7] Roe, David B.; Wilpon, Jay G. (1994). *Voice communication between humans and machines* (http://books.google.com/ books?id=UUDcUnmVVMYC&pg=PA19&dq=digital microelectronics&f=false). U.S. National Academy of Science Press. p. 19. ISBN 0309049887. . "...microelectronics technology."

[8] Chen, Wai-Kai (2005). *The electrical engineering handbook* (http://books.google.com/books?id=qhHsSlazGrQC&pg=PA101& dq=analog-digital+noise#v=onepage&q=analog-digital noise&f=false). Academic Press. p. 101. ISBN 0121709600. . "Noise from an analog (or small-signal) perspective..."

[9] Scherz, Paul (2006). *Practical electronics for inventors* (http://books.google.com/books?id=nMBtypLEdqgC&pg=PA730&dq=analog+ to+digital+converter#v=onepage&q=analog to digital converter&f=false). McGraw-Hill Professional. p. 730. ISBN 0071452816. . "In order for analog devices... to communicate with digital circuits..."

[10] Williams, Jim (1991). *Analog circuit design* (http://books.google.com/books?id=CFoEAP2lwLEC&pg=PA238&dq=analog+circuit+ design+difficulty#v=onepage&q=analog circuit design difficulty&f=false). Newnes. p. 238. ISBN 0750696401. . "Even within companies producing both analog and digital products..."

Linear

The word **linear** comes from the Latin word *linearis*, which means *created by lines*. In mathematics, a linear map or function $f(x)$ is a function which satisfies the following two properties:

- Additivity (also called the superposition property): $f(x + y) = f(x) + f(y)$. This says that f is a group homomorphism with respect to addition.
- Homogeneity of degree 1: $f(\alpha x) = \alpha f(x)$ for all α.

It can be shown that additivity implies the homogeneity in all cases where α is rational; this is done by proving the case where α is a natural number by mathematical induction and then extending the result to arbitrary rational numbers. If f is assumed to be continuous as well then this can be extended to show that homogeneity for α any real number, using the fact the rationals form a dense subset of the reals.

In this definition, x is not necessarily a real number, but can in general be a member of any vector space. A less restrictive definition of linear function, not coinciding with the definition of linear map, is used in elementary mathematics.

The concept of linearity can be extended to linear operators. Important examples of linear operators include the derivative considered as a differential operator, and many constructed from it, such as del and the Laplacian. When a differential equation can be expressed in linear form, it is particularly easy to solve by breaking the equation up into smaller pieces, solving each of those pieces, and adding the solutions up.

Linear algebra is the branch of mathematics concerned with the study of vectors, vector spaces (also called linear spaces), linear transformations (also called linear maps), and systems of linear equations.

If you are looking for an explanation of what linear and nonlinear equations are, please see Linear equation. Nonlinear equations and functions are of interest to physicists and mathematicians because they can be used to represent many natural phenomena, including chaos.

Integral linearity

For a device that converts a quantity to another quantity there are three basic definitions for integral linearity in common use: independent linearity, zero-based linearity, and terminal, or end-point, linearity. In each case, linearity defines how well the device's actual performance across a specified operating range approximates a straight line. Linearity is usually measured in terms of a deviation, or non-linearity, from an ideal straight line and it is typically expressed in terms of percent of full scale, or in ppm (parts per million) of full scale. Typically, the straight line is obtained by performing a least-squares fit of the data. The three definitions vary in the manner in which the straight line is positioned relative to the actual device's performance. Also, all three of these definitions ignore any gain, or offset errors that may be present in the actual device's performance characteristics.

Many times a device's specifications will simply refer to linearity, with no other explanation as to which type of linearity is intended. In cases where a specification is expressed simply as linearity, it is assumed to imply independent linearity.

Independent linearity is probably the most commonly-used linearity definition and is often found in the specifications for DMMs and ADCs, as well as devices like potentiometers. Independent linearity is defined as the maximum deviation of actual performance relative to a straight line, located such that it minimizes the maximum deviation. In that case there are no constraints placed upon the positioning of the straight line and it may be wherever necessary to minimize the deviations between it and the device's actual performance characteristic.

Zero-based linearity forces the lower range value of the straight line to be equal to the actual lower range value of the device's characteristic, but it does allow the line to be rotated to minimize the maximum deviation. In this case, since the positioning of the straight line is constrained by the requirement that the lower range values of the line and the device's characteristic be coincident, the non-linearity based on this definition will generally be larger than for independent linearity.

For terminal linearity, there is no flexibility allowed in the placement of the straight line in order to minimize the deviations. The straight line must be located such that each of its end-points coincides with the device's actual upper and lower range values. This means that the non-linearity measured by this definition will typically be larger than that measured by the independent, or the zero-based linearity definitions. This definition of linearity is often associated with ADCs, DACs and various sensors.

A fourth linearity definition, absolute linearity, is sometimes also encountered. Absolute linearity is a variation of terminal linearity, in that it allows no flexibility in the placement of the straight line, however in this case the gain and offset errors of the actual device are included in the linearity measurement, making this the most difficult measure of a device's performance. For absolute linearity the end points of the straight line are defined by the ideal upper and lower range values for the device, rather than the actual values. The linearity error in this instance is the maximum deviation of the actual device's performance from ideal.

Linear polynomials

In a different usage to the above, a polynomial of degree 1 is said to be linear, because the graph of a function of that form is a line.

Over the reals, a linear equation is one of the form:

$$f(x) = mx + b$$

where m is often called the slope or gradient; b the y-intercept, which gives the point of intersection between the graph of the function and the y-axis.

Note that this usage of the term *linear* is not the same as the above, because linear polynomials over the real numbers do not in general satisfy either additivity or homogeneity. In fact, they do so if and only if $b = 0$. Hence, if $b \neq 0$, the function is often called an **affine function** (see in greater generality affine transformation).

Boolean functions

In Boolean algebra, a linear function is a function f for which there exist $a_0, a_1, \ldots, a_n \in \{0, 1\}$ such that

$$f(b_1, \ldots, b_n) = a_0 \oplus (a_1 \wedge b_1) \oplus \ldots \oplus (a_n \wedge b_n) \text{for all } b_1, \ldots, b_n \in \{0, 1\}.$$

A Boolean function is linear if A) In every row of the truth table in which the value of the function is 'T', there are an even number of 'T's assigned to the arguments of the function; and in every row in which the truth value of the function is 'F', there are an odd number of 'T's assigned to arguments; or B) In every row in which the truth value of the function is 'T', there are an odd number of 'T's assigned to the arguments and in every row in which the function is 'F' there is an even number of 'T's assigned to arguments.

Another way to express this is that each variable always makes a difference in the truth-value of the operation or it never makes a difference.

Negation, Logical biconditional, exclusive or, tautology, and contradiction are linear functions.

Physics

In physics, *linearity* is a property of the differential equations governing many systems. For instance, Maxwell equations or the diffusion equation.

Linearity of a differential equation means that if two functions *f* and *g* are solution of the equation, then their sum *f*+*g* is also a solution of the equation.

Electronics

In electronics, the linear operating region of a transistor is where the collector-emitter current is related to the base current by a simple scale factor, enabling the transistor to be used as an amplifier that preserves the fidelity of analog signals. Linear is similarly used to describe regions of any function, mathematical or physical, that follow a straight line with arbitrary slope.

Such linear electronic devices include linear filter, linear regulator, linear amplifier.

Military tactical formations

In military tactical formations, "linear formations" were adapted from phalanx-like formations of pike protected by handgunners towards shallow formations of handgunners protected by progressively fewer pikes. This kind of formation would get thinner until its extreme in the age of Wellington with the 'Thin Red Line'. It would eventually be replaced by skirmish order at the time of the invention of the breech-loading rifle that allowed soldiers to move and fire independently of the large scale formations and fight in small, mobile units.

Art

Linear is one of the five categories proposed by Swiss art historian Heinrich Wölfflin to distinguish "Classic", or Renaissance art, from the Baroque. According to Wölfflin, painters of the fifteenth and early sixteenth centuries (Leonardo da Vinci, Raphael or Albrecht Dürer) are more linear than "painterly" Baroque painters of the seventeenth century (Peter Paul Rubens, Rembrandt, and Velázquez) because they primarily use outline to create shape.[1] Linearity in art can also be referenced in digital art. For example, hypertext fiction can be an example of nonlinear narrative, but there are also websites designed to go in a specified, organized manner, following a linear path.

Music

In music the **linear** aspect is succession, either intervals or melody, as opposed to simultaneity or the vertical aspect.

Measurement

In measurement, the term "linear foot" refers to the number of feet in a straight line of material (such as lumber or fabric) generally without regard to the width. It is sometimes incorrectly referred to as "lineal feet"; however, "lineal" is typically reserved for usage when referring to ancestry or heredity.[2] The words "linear"[3] & "lineal" [4] both descend from the same root meaning, the Latin word for line, which is "linea".

See also

- Linear element
- Linear system
- Linear medium
- Linear programming
- Bilinear
- Multilinear
- Linear motor
- Linear A and Linear B scripts.
- Linear interpolation

References

[1] Heinrich Wölfflin, *Principles of Art History: the Problem of the Development of Style in Later Art*, M. D. Hottinger (trans.), Mineola, N.Y.: Dover (1950): pp. 18-72.

Schematic capture

Schematic capture or **schematic entry** is a step in the design cycle of electronic design automation (EDA) at which the electronic diagram, or electronic schematic of the designed electronic circuit is created by a designer. This is done interactively with the help of a schematic capture tool also known as schematic editor.

Orcad schematic capture program

The circuit design is the very first step of actual design of an electronic circuit. Typically sketches are drawn on paper, and then entered into a computer using a schematic editor. Therefore schematic entry is said to be a front-end operation of several others in the design flow.

Despite the complexity of modern components – huge ball grid arrays and tiny passive components – schematic capture is easier today than it has been for many years. CAD software is easier to use and is available in full-featured expensive packages, very capable mid-range packages that sometimes have free versions and completely free versions that are either open source or directly linked to a printed circuit board fabrication company.

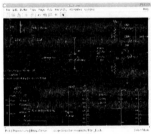

gschem open source schematic capture. Part of the gEDA suite

In past years, schematic diagrams with largely discrete components were fairly readable however with the newer high pin-count parts and with the almost universal use of standard letter-sized paper, schematics have become less so. Many times, there will be a single large part on a page with nothing but pin reference keys to connect it to other pages.

Readability levels can be enhanced by using buses and superbuses, related pins can be connected into a common bus and routed to other pages. Buses don't need to be just the traditional address or data bus directly linked pins. A bus grouping can also be used for related uses, such as all analog input or all communications related pin functions.

Other Considerations

After the circuit design is captured in a schematic, most EDA tools allow the design to be simulated.

Schematic capture involves not only entering the circuits into the CAD system, but also generally calls for decisions that may seem more appropriate for later in the design, such as package choice. Although you may be able to change the package later, many PCB CAD systems ask you to choose both the part and package when placing it into the schematic capture program.

This also brings into play such considerations as prototyping and assembly. In a high-volume assembly environment, there will be plenty of opportunities for DFM analysis. However, in a rapid prototyping environment such as at assembly houses specializing in low-volume/high-mix and quick turnaround times, the pick and place machines are programmed directly from the board layout files. Careful package selection during schematic capture will save time during the assembly and debug process.

With new parts, the CAD system may not have your chosen component in its parts library, so you may need to create the parts library yourself. Again, you may at the time not be overly concerned with the package, but careful creation of the part library will save time and risk later.

After the circuit design is captured in a schematic, then the PCB layout can begin.

Schematic Capture Tips

To make schematics easier to read there are a few tips that can increase organization and readability.

- Schematics should read left to right, just like a book. Generally, inputs on the left, outputs on the right.
- Naming signals / nets will dramatically increase the readability and traceability of your schematics. It will be a great help during the pcb design phase of your project.
- No 4-way ties. A 4-way tie can cause confusion and should be avoided at all times (This 'tip' is often contended among design professionals).
- Break the schematic into logical building blocks. This is easily accomplished with multiple pages, each having a dedicated functionality.
- Use all capital letters as much as possible, especially for small text such as net names. This improves legibility, and is required by most drafting standards.
- To maximize portability, net names should consist of letters, numbers, and underscores. Use of characters such as spaces, pluses or minuses, or case sensitive names (i.e. two or more names who only differ in case) is discouraged, as it can cause subtle problems when exporting a netlist for simulation or layout. For example, net names in Verilog cannot have spaces; a netlist export tool would have to "escape" these characters to allow a Verilog simulation, which could lead to confusion if there are later errors referencing these nets.

See also

- Comparison of EDA software
- Comparison of Free EDA software

Individual products

- Altium – Providers of Altium Designer (formerly Protel) and P-CAD (retired June 30, 2008).
- Autotrax – EDA/DEX is a Windows XP/Vista/7 schematic capture / PCB design layout program with built in Spice simulator and 3D part and board visualization.
- DipTrace – mid-range Schematic Capture and PCB Layout software that has a free version.
- Edwinxp – Totally Integrated Schematic Capture, Simulation and PCB design software.
- Electronics Workbench – Schematic Capture, Simulation and PCB design software suite.

- Multisim – Schematic Capture and SPICE Simulation software.
- Cadsoft EAGLE – Very capable mid-range Schematic Capture software that has a free version.
- Kicad – open source schematic capture and PCB design software suite
- OrCAD – Full-featured commercial Schematic Capture and PCB layout.
- TARGET 3001! – mid-range Schematic Capture software that has a free version.
- gEDA – open source schematic capture using gschem, simulation, and PCB design software suite
- The Electric VLSI Design System

References

- Pratt, Gary; Jarrett, Jay (August 6, 2001), "Top-Down Design Methods Bring Back The Useful Schematic Diagram" [1], *Electronic Design* **49** (16): 69–unknown, ISSN 0013-4872, ED Online ID #3784.

External links

- The importance of 'Schematic Readiness', and their portability. [2]
- Tips for marking SMT LEDs and diodes for accurate PCB assembly [3] by Screaming Circuits

SapWin

Developer(s)	University of Florence
Stable release	3.0 build 1.57 / December 2008
Written in	C++
Operating system	Microsoft Windows
Available in	English
Type	Electronic design automation
Website	cirlab.det.unifi.it/Sapwin/ [1]

SAPWIN (Symbolic Analysis Program for Windows) is a symbolic circuit simulator written in C++ for the Windows (95/98/ME/NT/2000) environment. Unlike more common numerical circuit simulators (such as SPICE), SAPWIN can generate analytical Laplace domain expressions for arbitrary network functions of linear analog circuits. The SAPWIN package also includes tools for schematic capture and graphic post-processing.

SAPWIN is available free from its homepage at the University of Florence website.

SAPEC-NG

SAPEC-NG (Symbolic Analysis Program for Electric Circuits - Next Generation) is the open-source successor to SAPWIN, written in C and designed for the Linux platform. It is currently in development and lacks schematic capture and a GUI front-end.

See also

- SNAP
- Symbolic Circuit Analysis

External links

- SAPWIN screenshot [2]
- SAPWIN - A Symbolic Simulator as a Support in Electrical Engineering Education [3]
- SAPEC-NG [4]

Symbolic Circuit Analysis

Symbolic circuit analysis is a formal technique of circuit analysis to calculate the behaviour or characteristic of an electric/electronic circuit with the independent variables (time or frequency), the dependent variables (voltages and currents), and (some or all of) the circuit elements represented by symbols.[1]

When analysing electric/electronic circuits, we may ask two types of questions: What is the **value** of certain circuit variable (voltage, current, resistance, gain, etc.) or what is the **relationship** between some circuit variables or between a circuit variable and circuit components and frequency (or time). Such relationship may take the form of a graph, where numerical values of a circuit variable are plotted versus frequency or component value (the most common example would be a plot of the magnitude of a transfer function vs. frequency).

Symbolic circuit analysis is concerned with obtaining those relationships in symbolic form, i.e., in the form of analytical expression, where the complex frequency (or time) and some or all of the circuit components are represented by symbols.

Frequency domain expressions

In the frequency domain the most common task of symbolic circuit analysis is to obtain the relationship between input and output variables in the form of a rational function in the complex frequency s and symbolic variables $\mathbf{X}$:

$$T(s, \mathbf{x}) = \frac{N(s, \mathbf{x})}{D(s, \mathbf{x})}$$

The above relationship is often called the network function. For physical systems, $N(s, \mathbf{x})$ and $D(s, \mathbf{x})$ are polynomials in s with real coefficients:

$$T(s, \mathbf{x}) = \frac{\sum_{i=0}^{n} a_i(\mathbf{x})s^i}{\sum_{i=0}^{m} b_i(\mathbf{x})s^i} = K \frac{\prod_{i=1}^{n}(s - z_i(\mathbf{x}))}{\prod_{i=1}^{m}(s - p_i(\mathbf{x}))}$$

where $z_i(\mathbf{x})$ are the zeroes and $p_i(\mathbf{x})$ are the poles of the network function; $m \geqslant n$.

While there are several methods for generating coefficients $a_i(\mathbf{x})$ and $b_i(\mathbf{x})$, no technique exists to obtain exact symbolic expressions for poles and zeroes for polynomials of order higher than 5.

Types of symbolic network functions

Depending on which parameters are kept as symbols, we may have several different types of symbolic network functions. This is best illustrated on an example. Consider, for instance, the biquad filter circuit with ideal op amps, shown below. We want to obtain a formula for its voltage transmittance (also called the voltage gain) in the frequency domain, $T_v(s) = V_{out}(s)/V_{in}(s)$.

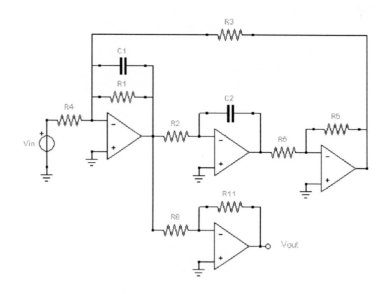

Figure 1: Biquad circuit with ideal opamps. (This diagram was created using the schematic capture feature of SapWin.)

Network function with s as the only variable

If the complex frequency s is the only variable, the formula will look like this (for simplicity we use the numerical values: $R_i = i, C_i = 0.01i$):

$$T(s) = \frac{3.48s}{13.2s^2 + 1.32s + 0.33}$$

Semi-symbolic network function

If the complex frequency s and some circuit variables are kept as symbols (semi-symbolic analysis), the formula may take a form:

$$T(s, \mathbf{x}) = \frac{1.74C_2s}{6.6C_1C_2s^2 + 0.66C_2s + 0.33}$$
$$\mathbf{x} = [C_1 \ C_2]$$

Fully symbolic netwok function

If the complex frequency s and all circuit variables are symbolic (fully symbolic analysis), the voltage transmittance is given by (here $G_i = 1/R_i$):

$$T(s, \mathbf{x}) = \frac{G_4 G_6 G_8 C_2 s}{G_6 G_{11} C_1 C_2 s^2 + G_1 G_6 G_{11} C_2 s + G_2 G_3 G_5 G_{11}}$$

$$\mathbf{x} = [C_1 \ C_2 \ G_1 \ G_2 \ G_3 \ G_4 \ G_5 \ G_6 \ G_8 \ G_{11}]$$

All expressions above are extremely useful in obtaining insight into operation of the circuit and understanding how each component contributes to the overall circuit performance. As the circuit size increases, however, the number of terms in such expressions grows exponentially. So, even for relatively simple circuits, the formulae become too long to be of any practical value. One way to deal with this problem is to omit insignificant terms from the symbolic expression, keeping the inevitable error below the predetermined limit.[2]

Sequence of Expressions form

Another possibility to shorten the symbolic expression to manageable length is to represent the network function by a sequence of expressions (SoE)[3] . Of course, the interpretability of the formula is lost, but this approach is very useful for repetitive numerical calculations. There are several types of SoE, that can be obtained. For example, the compact SoE for $T_v(s)$ of our biquad is

```
x1 = G5*G3/G6
x2 = -G1-s*C1-G2*x1/(s*C2)
x3 = -G4*G8/x2
Ts = x3/G11
```

The above sequence contains fractions. If this is not desirable (when divisions by zero appear, for instance), we may generate a fractionless SoE:

```
x1 = -G2*G5
x2 = G6*s*C2
x3 = -G4*x2
x4 = x1*G3-(G1+s*C1)*x2
x5 = x3*G8
x6 = -G11*x4
Ts = -x5/x6
```

Yet another way to shorten the expression is to factorise polynomials $N(s, \mathbf{x})$ and $D(s, \mathbf{x})$. For our example this is very simple and leads to:

```
Num = G4*G6*G8*s*C2
Den = G11*((G1+s*C1)*G6*s*C2+G2*G3*C5)
Ts = Num/Den
```

For larger circuits, however, factorisation becomes a difficult combinatorial problem and the final result may be impractical for both interpretation and numerical calculations.

External links

- Library of benchmark circuits for symbolic circuit analysis [4]
- SapWin 3.0 - software for symbolic circuit analysis [1]
- SNAP - software for symbolic, semisymbolic and numerical circuit analysis [2]

References

[1] G. Gielen and W. Sansen, Symbolic Analysis for Automated Design of Analog Integrated Circuits. Boston: Kluwer Academic Publishers, 1991.

[2] B. Rodanski, M. Hassoun, "Symbolic Analysis," in The Circuits and Filters Handbook: Fundamentals of Circuits and Filters, 3rd ed., Wai-Kai Chen, Editor. CRC Press, 2009, pp. 25-1 - 25-29.

[3] M. Pierzchala, B. Rodanski, "Generation of Sequential Symbolic Network Functions for Large-Scale Networks by Circuit Reduction to a Two-Port," IEEE Transactions on Circuits and Systems - I: Fundamental Theory and Applications, vol. 48, no. 7, July 2001, pp. 906-909.

Laplace

Pierre-Simon, marquis de Laplace	

Pierre-Simon Laplace (1749–1827). Posthumous portrait by Madame Feytaud, 1842.	
Born	23 March 1749 Beaumont-en-Auge, Normandy, France
Died	5 March 1827 (aged 77) Paris, France
Residence	France
Nationality	French
Fields	Astronomer and Mathematician
Institutions	École Militaire (1769–1776)
Alma mater	University of Caen
Academic advisors	Jean d'Alembert Christophe Gadbled Pierre Le Canu
Doctoral students	Simeon Denis Poisson
Known for	Work in Celestial Mechanics Laplace's equation Laplacian Laplace transform Laplace distribution Laplace's demon Laplace expansion Young–Laplace equation Laplace number Laplace limit Laplace invariant Laplace principle

Pierre-Simon, marquis de Laplace (23 March 1749 – 5 March 1827) was a French mathematician and astronomer whose work was pivotal to the development of mathematical astronomy and statistics. He summarized and extended the work of his predecessors in his five volume *Mécanique Céleste* (Celestial Mechanics) (1799–1825). This work translated the geometric study of classical mechanics to one based on calculus, opening up a broader range of problems. In statistics, the so-called Bayesian interpretation of probability was mainly developed by Laplace.[1]

He formulated Laplace's equation, and pioneered the Laplace transform which appears in many branches of mathematical physics, a field that he took a leading role in forming. The Laplacian differential operator, widely used in applied mathematics, is also named after him.

He restated and developed the nebular hypothesis of the origin of the solar system and was one of the first scientists to postulate the existence of black holes and the notion of gravitational collapse.

He is remembered as one of the greatest scientists of all time, sometimes referred to as a *French Newton* or *Newton of France*, with a phenomenal natural mathematical faculty superior to any of his contemporaries.[2]

He became a count of the First French Empire in 1806 and was named a marquis in 1817, after the Bourbon Restoration.

Early life

Many details of the life of Laplace were lost when the family château burned in 1925.[3] Laplace was born in Beaumont-en-Auge, Normandy in 1749. According to W. W. Rouse Ball (*A Short Account of the History of Mathematics*, 4th edition, 1908), he was the son of a small cottager or perhaps a farm-labourer, and owed his education to the interest excited in some wealthy neighbours by his abilities and engaging presence. Very little is known of his early years. It would seem from a pupil he became an usher in the school at Beaumont; but, having procured a letter of introduction to d'Alembert, he went to Paris to push his fortune. However, Karl Pearson[3] is scathing about the inaccuracies in Rouse Ball's account and states,

> Indeed Caen was probably in Laplace's day the most intellectually active of all the towns of Normandy. It was here that Laplace was educated and was provisionally a professor. It was here he wrote his first paper published in the *Mélanges* of the Royal Society of Turin, Tome iv. 1766–1769, at least two years before he went at 22 or 23 to Paris in 1771. Thus before he was 20 he was in touch with Lagrange in Turin. He did not go to Paris a raw self-taught country lad with only a peasant background! In 1765 at the age of sixteen Laplace left the "School of the Duke of Orleans" in Beaumont and went to the University of Caen, where he appears to have studied for five years. The 'Ecole militaire' of Beaumont did not replace the old school until 1776.

His parents were from comfortable families. His father was Pierre Laplace, and his mother was Marie-Anne Sochon. The Laplace family was involved in agriculture until at least 1750, but Pierre Laplace senior was also a cider merchant and *syndic* of the town of Beaumont.

Pierre Simon Laplace attended a school in the village run at a Benedictine priory, his father intending that he would be ordained in the Roman Catholic Church, and at sixteen he was sent to further his father's intention at the University of Caen, reading theology.[4]

At the university, he was mentored by two enthusiastic teachers of mathematics, Christophe Gadbled and Pierre Le Canu, who awoke his zeal for the subject. Laplace never graduated in theology but left for Paris with a letter of introduction from Le Canu to Jean le Rond d'Alembert.[4]

According to his great-great-grandson,[3] d'Alembert received him rather poorly, and to get rid of him gave him a thick mathematics book, saying to come back when he had read it. When Laplace came back a few days later, d'Alembert was even less friendly and did not hide his opinion that it was impossible that Laplace could have read and understood the book. But upon questioning him, he realized that it was true, and from that time he took Laplace under his care.

Another version is that Laplace solved overnight a problem that d'Alembert set him for submission the following week, then solved a harder problem the following night. D'Alembert was impressed and recommended him for a teaching place in the *École Militaire*.[5]

With a secure income and undemanding teaching, Laplace now threw himself into original research and, in the next seventeen years, 1771–1787, he produced much of his original work in astronomy.[6]

Laplace further impressed the Marquis de Condorcet, and even in 1771 Laplace felt that he was entitled to membership in the French Academy of Sciences. However, in that year, admission went to Alexandre-Théophile Vandermonde and in 1772 to Jacques Antoine Joseph Cousin. Laplace was disgruntled, and at the beginning of

1773, d'Alembert wrote to Lagrange in Berlin to ask if a position could be found for Laplace there. However, Condorcet became permanent secretary of the *Académie* in February and Laplace was elected associate member on 31 March, at age 24.[7]

He married Marie-Charlotte de Courty de Romanges in his late thirties and the couple had a daughter, Sophie, and a son, Charles-Émile (b. 1789).[3] [8]

Analysis, probability and astronomical stability

Laplace's early published work in 1771 started with differential equations and finite differences but he was already starting to think about the mathematical and philosophical concepts of probability and statistics.[9] However, before his election to the *Académie* in 1773, he had already drafted two papers that would establish his reputation. The first, *Mémoire sur la probabilité des causes par les événements* was ultimately published in 1774 while the second paper, published in 1776, further elaborated his statistical thinking and also began his systematic work on celestial mechanics and the stability of the solar system. The two disciplines would always be interlinked in his mind. "Laplace took probability as an instrument for repairing defects in knowledge."[10] Laplace's work on probability and statistics is discussed below with his mature work on the Analytic theory of probabilities.

Stability of the solar system

Sir Isaac Newton had published his *Philosophiae Naturalis Principia Mathematica* in 1687 in which he gave a derivation of Kepler's laws, which describe the motion of the planets, from his laws of motion and his law of universal gravitation. However, though Newton had privately developed the methods of calculus, all his published work used cumbersome geometric reasoning, unsuitable to account for the more subtle higher-order effects of interactions between the planets. Newton himself had doubted the possibility of a mathematical solution to the whole, even concluding that periodic divine intervention was necessary to guarantee the stability of the solar system. Dispensing with the hypothesis of divine intervention would be a major activity of Laplace's scientific life.[11] It is now generally regarded that Laplace's methods on their own, though vital to the development of the theory, are not sufficiently precise to demonstrate the stability of the Solar System,[12] and indeed, the Solar System is now understood to be chaotic, although it actually appears to be fairly stable.

One particular problem from observational astronomy was the apparent instability whereby Jupiter's orbit appeared to be shrinking while that of Saturn was expanding. The problem had been tackled by Leonhard Euler in 1748 and Joseph Louis Lagrange in 1763 but without success.[13] In 1776, Laplace published a memoir in which he first explored the possible influences of a purported luminiferous ether or of a law of gravitation that did not act instantaneously. He ultimately returned to an intellectual investment in Newtonian gravity.[14] Euler and Lagrange had made a practical approximation by ignoring small terms in the equations of motion. Laplace noted that though the terms themselves were small, when integrated over time they could become important. Laplace carried his analysis into the higher-order terms, up to and including the cubic. Using this more exact analysis, Laplace concluded that any two planets and the sun must be in mutual equilibrium and thereby launched his work on the stability of the solar system.[15] Gerald James Whitrow described the achievement as "the most important advance in physical astronomy since Newton".[11]

Laplace had a wide knowledge of all sciences and dominated all discussions in the *Académie*.[16] Laplace seems to have regarded analysis merely as a means of attacking physical problems, though the ability with which he invented the necessary analysis is almost phenomenal. As long as his results were true he took but little trouble to explain the steps by which he arrived at them; he never studied elegance or symmetry in his processes, and it was sufficient for him if he could by any means solve the particular question he was discussing.[6]

On the figure of the Earth

During the years 1784–1787 he published some memoirs of exceptional power. Prominent among these is one read in 1783, reprinted as Part II of *Théorie du Mouvement et de la figure elliptique des planètes* in 1784, and in the third volume of the *Méchanique céleste*. In this work, Laplace completely determined the attraction of a spheroid on a particle outside it. This is memorable for the introduction into analysis of spherical harmonics or **Laplace's coefficients**, and also for the development of the use of the potential, a name first used by George Green in 1828.[6]

Spherical harmonics

In 1783, in a paper sent to the *Académie*, Adrien-Marie Legendre had introduced what are now known as associated Legendre functions.[6] If two points in a plane have polar co-ordinates (r, θ) and (r', θ'), where $r' \geq r$, then, by elementary manipulation, the reciprocal of the distance between the points, d, can be written as:

Spherical harmonics

$$\frac{1}{d} = \frac{1}{r'} \left[1 - 2\cos(\theta' - \theta)\frac{r}{r'} + \left(\frac{r}{r'}\right)^2 \right]^{-\frac{1}{2}}.$$

This expression can be expanded in powers of r/r' using Newton's generalized binomial theorem to give:

$$\frac{1}{d} = \frac{1}{r'} \sum_{k=0}^{\infty} P_k^0(\cos(\theta' - \theta)) \left(\frac{r}{r'}\right)^k.$$

The sequence of functions $P_k^0(\cos\phi)$ is the set of so-called "associated Legendre functions" and their usefulness arises from the fact that every function of the points on a circle can be expanded as a series of them.[6]

Laplace, with scant regard for credit to Legendre, made the non-trivial extension of the result to three dimensions to yield a more general set of functions, the **spherical harmonics** or **Laplace coefficients**. The latter term is not now in common use. Every function of the points on a sphere can be expanded as a series of them.[6]

Potential theory

This paper is also remarkable for the development of the idea of the scalar potential.[6] The gravitational force acting on a body is, in modern language, a vector, having magnitude and direction. A potential function is a scalar function that defines how the vectors will behave. A scalar function is computationally and conceptually easier to deal with than a vector function.

Alexis Clairault had first suggested the idea in 1743 while working on a similar problem though he was using Newtonian-type geometric reasoning. Laplace described Clairault's work as being "in the class of the most beautiful mathematical productions".[17] However, Rouse Ball alleges that the idea "was appropriated from Joseph Louis Lagrange, who had used it in his memoirs of 1773, 1777 and 1780".[6]

Laplace applied the language of calculus to the potential function and shows that it always satisfies the differential equation:[6]

$$\nabla^2 V = \frac{\partial^2 V}{\partial x^2} + \frac{\partial^2 V}{\partial y^2} + \frac{\partial^2 V}{\partial z^2} = 0.$$

His subsequent work on gravitational attraction was based on this result. The quantity $\nabla^2 V$ has been termed the **concentration** of V and its value at any point indicates the "excess" of the value of V there over its mean value in the neighbourhood of the point. Laplace's equation, a special case of Poisson's equation, appears ubiquitously in mathematical physics. The concept of a potential occurs in fluid dynamics, electromagnetism and other areas. Rouse Ball speculated that it might be seen as "the outward sign" of one the "*prior* forms" in Kant's theory of perception.[6]
The spherical harmonics turn out to be critical to practical solutions of Laplace's equation. Laplace's equation in spherical coordinates, such as are used for mapping the sky, can be simplified, using the method of separation of variables into a radial part, depending solely on distance from the centre point, and an angular or spherical part. The solution to the spherical part of the equation can be expressed as a series of Laplace's spherical harmonics, simplifying practical computation.

Planetary and lunar inequalities

Jupiter-Saturn great inequality

Laplace presented a memoir on planetary inequalities in three sections, in 1784, 1785, and 1786. This dealt mainly with the identification and explanation of the perturbations now known as the "great Jupiter-Saturn inequality". Laplace solved a longstanding problem in the study and prediction of the movements of these planets. He showed by general considerations, first, that the mutual action of two planets could never cause large changes in the eccentricities and inclinations of their orbits; but then, even more importantly, that peculiarities arose in the Jupiter-Saturn system because of the near approach to commensurability of the mean motions of Jupiter and Saturn. (Commensurability, in this context, means related by ratios of small whole numbers. Two periods of Saturn's orbit around the Sun almost equal five of Jupiter's. The corresponding difference between multiples of the mean motions, $(2n_J - 5n_S)$, corresponds to a period of nearly 900 years, and it occurs as a small divisor in the integration of a very small perturbing force with this same period. As a result, the integrated perturbations with this period are disproportionately large, about 0.8° (degrees of arc in orbital longitude) for Saturn and about 0.3° for Jupiter.) Further developments of these theorems on planetary motion were given in his two memoirs of 1788 and 1789, but with the aid of Laplace's discoveries, the tables of the motions of Jupiter and Saturn could at last be made much more accurate. It was on the basis of Laplace's theory that Delambre computed his astronomical tables.[6]

Lunar inequalities

Laplace also produced an analytical solution (as it turned out later, a partial solution), to a significant problem regarding the motion of the Moon. Edmond Halley had been the first to suggest, in 1695,[18] that the mean motion of the Moon was apparently getting faster, by comparison with ancient eclipse observations, but he gave no data. (It was not yet known in Halley's or Laplace's times that what is actually occurring includes a slowing-down of the Earth's rate of rotation: see also Ephemeris time - History. When measured as a function of mean solar time rather than uniform time, the effect appears as a positive acceleration.) In 1749 Richard Dunthorne confirmed Halley's suspicion after re-examining ancient records, and produced the first quantitative estimate for the size of this apparent effect:[19] a centurial rate of +10" (arcseconds) in lunar longitude (a surprisingly good result for its time, not far different from values assessed later, e.g. in 1786 by de Lalande[20] , and to compare with values from about 10" to nearly 13" being derived about century later.)[21] [22] The effect became known as the *secular acceleration of the Moon*, but until Laplace, its cause remained unknown.

Laplace gave an explanation of the effect in 1787, showing how an acceleration arises from changes (a secular reduction) in the eccentricity of the Earth's orbit, which in turn is one of the effects of planetary perturbations on the Earth. Laplace's initial computation accounted for the whole effect, thus seeming to tie up the theory neatly with both modern and ancient observations. However, in 1853, J C Adams caused the question to be re-opened by finding an error in Laplace's computations: it turned out that only about half of the Moon's apparent acceleration could be accounted for on Laplace's basis by the change in the Earth's orbital eccentricity.[23] (Adams showed that Laplace had in effect only considered the radial force on the moon and not the tangential, and the partial result hence had overstimated the acceleration, the remaining (negative), terms when accounted for, showed that Laplace's cause could not explain more than about half of the acceleration. The other half was subsequently shown to be due to tidal acceleration.[24])

Laplace used his results concerning the lunar acceleration when completing his attempted "proof" of the stability of the whole solar system on the assumption that it consists of a collection of rigid bodies moving in a vacuum.[6]

All the memoirs above alluded to were presented to the *Académie des sciences*, and they are printed in the *Mémoires présentés par divers savants*.[6]

Celestial mechanics

Laplace now set himself the task to write a work which should "offer a complete solution of the great mechanical problem presented by the solar system, and bring theory to coincide so closely with observation that empirical equations should no longer find a place in astronomical tables." The result is embodied in the *Exposition du système du monde* and the *Mécanique céleste*.[6]

The former was published in 1796, and gives a general explanation of the phenomena, but omits all details. It contains a summary of the history of astronomy. This summary procured for its author the honour of admission to the forty of the French Academy and is commonly esteemed one of the masterpieces of French literature, though it is not altogether reliable for the later periods of which it treats.[6]

Laplace developed the nebular hypothesis of the formation of the solar system, first suggested by Emanuel Swedenborg and expanded by Immanuel Kant, a hypothesis that continues to dominate accounts of the origin of planetary systems. According to Laplace's description of the hypothesis, the solar system had evolved from a globular mass of incandescent gas rotating around an axis through its centre of mass. As it cooled, this mass contracted, and successive rings broke off from its outer edge. These rings in their turn cooled, and finally condensed into the planets, while the sun represented the central core which was still left. On this view, Laplace predicted that the more distant planets would be older than those nearer the sun.[6] [25]

As mentioned, the idea of the nebular hypothesis had been outlined by Immanuel Kant in 1755,[25] and he had also suggested "meteoric aggregations" and tidal friction as causes affecting the formation of the solar system. Laplace was probably aware of this, but, like many writers of his time, he generally did not reference the work of others.[3]

Laplace's analytical discussion of the solar system is given in his *Méchanique céleste* published in five volumes. The first two volumes, published in 1799, contain methods for calculating the motions of the planets, determining their figures, and resolving tidal problems. The third and fourth volumes, published in 1802 and 1805, contain applications of these methods, and several astronomical tables. The fifth volume, published in 1825, is mainly historical, but it gives as appendices the results of Laplace's latest researches. Laplace's own investigations embodied in it are so numerous and valuable that it is regrettable to have to add that many results are appropriated from other writers with scanty or no acknowledgement, and the conclusions – which have been described as the organized result of a century of patient toil – are frequently mentioned as if they were due to Laplace.[6]

Jean-Baptiste Biot, who assisted Laplace in revising it for the press, says that Laplace himself was frequently unable to recover the details in the chain of reasoning, and, if satisfied that the conclusions were correct, he was content to insert the constantly recurring formula, "*Il est aisé à voir que...*" ("It is easy to see that..."). The *Mécanique céleste* is not only the translation of Newton's *Principia* into the language of the differential calculus, but it completes parts of which Newton had been unable to fill in the details. The work was carried forward in a more finely tuned form in Félix Tisserand's *Traité de mécanique céleste* (1889–1896), but Laplace's treatise will always remain a standard authority.[6]

Arcueil

In 1806, Laplace bought a house in Arcueil, then a village and not yet absorbed into the Paris conurbation. Claude Louis Berthollet was a near neighbour and the pair formed the nucleus of an informal scientific circle, latterly known as the Society of Arcueil. Because of their closeness to Napoleon, Laplace and Berthollet effectively controlled advancement in the scientific establishment and admission to the more prestigious offices. The Society built up a complex pyramid of patronage.[26] In 1806, he was also elected a foreign member of the Royal Swedish Academy of Sciences.

Laplace's house at Arcueil

Napoleon

An account of a famous interaction between Laplace and Napoleon is provided by Rouse Ball:[6]

> Laplace went in state to Napoleon to accept a copy of his work, and the following account of the interview is well authenticated, and so characteristic of all the parties concerned that I quote it in full. Someone had told Napoleon that the book contained no mention of the name of God; Napoleon, who was fond of putting embarrassing questions, received it with the remark, 'M. Laplace, they tell me you have written this large book on the system of the universe, and have never even mentioned its Creator.' Laplace, who, though the most supple of politicians, was as stiff as a martyr on every point of his philosophy, drew himself up and answered bluntly, 'Je n'avais pas besoin de cette hypothèse-là.' ("I had no need of that hypothesis.") Napoleon, greatly amused, told this reply to Lagrange, who exclaimed, 'Ah! c'est une belle hypothèse; ça explique beaucoup de choses.' ("Ah, it is a fine hypothesis; it explains many things.")

Black holes

Laplace also came close to propounding the concept of the black hole. He pointed out that there could be massive stars whose gravity is so great that not even light could escape from their surface (see escape velocity).[27] Laplace also speculated that some of the nebulae revealed by telescopes may not be part of the Milky Way and might actually be galaxies themselves. Thus, he anticipated Edwin Hubble's major discovery 100 years in advance.

Analytic theory of probabilities

In 1812, Laplace issued his *Théorie analytique des probabilités* in which he laid down many fundamental results in statistics. In 1819, he published a popular account of his work on probability. This book bears the same relation to the *Théorie des probabilités* that the *Système du monde* does to the *Méchanique céleste*.[6]

Probability-generating function

The method of estimating the ratio of the number of favourable cases, compared to the whole number of possible cases, had been previously indicated by Laplace in a paper written in 1779. It consists of treating the successive values of any function as the coefficients in the expansion of another function, with reference to a different variable. The latter is therefore called the probability-generating function of the former. Laplace then shows how, by means of interpolation, these coefficients may be determined from the generating function. Next he attacks the converse problem, and from the coefficients he finds the generating function; this is effected by the solution of a finite difference equation.[6]

Least squares

This treatise includes an exposition of the method of least squares, a remarkable testimony to Laplace's command over the processes of analysis. The method of least squares for the combination of numerous observations had been given empirically by Carl Friedrich Gauss (around 1794) and Legendre (in 1805), but the fourth chapter of this work contains a formal proof of it, on which the whole of the theory of errors has been since based. This was affected only by a most intricate analysis specially invented for the purpose, but the form in which it is presented is so meagre and unsatisfactory that, in spite of the uniform accuracy of the results, it was at one time questioned whether Laplace had actually gone through the difficult work he so briefly and often incorrectly indicates.[6]

Inductive probability

While he conducted much research in physics, another major theme of his life's endeavours was probability theory. In his *Essai philosophique sur les probabilités* (1814), Laplace set out a mathematical system of inductive reasoning based on probability, which we would today recognise as Bayesian. He begins the text with a series of principles of probability, the first six being:

1) Probability is the ratio of the "favored events" to the total possible events.

2) The first principle assumed equal probabilities for all events. When this is not true, we must first determine the probabilities of each event. Then, the probability is the sum of the probabilities of all possible favored events.

3) For independent events, the probability of the occurrence of all is the probability of each multiplied together.

4) For events not independent, the probability of event B following event A (or event A causing B) is the probability of A multiplied by the probability that A and B both occur.

5) The probability that A will occur, given B has occurred, is the probability of A and B occurring divided by the probability of B.

6) Three corollaries are given for the sixth principle, which amount to Bayesian probability. Where event $A_i \in \{A_1, A_2, ...A_n\}$ exhausts the list of possible causes for event B, $Pr(B) = Pr(A_1, A_2, ...A_n)$. Then

$$Pr(A_i|B) = \frac{Pr(B|A_i)}{\sum_i Pr(B|A_i)}.$$

One well-known formula arising from his system is the rule of succession, given as principle seven. Suppose that some trial has only two possible outcomes, labeled "success" and "failure". Under the assumption that little or nothing is known *a priori* about the relative plausibilities of the outcomes, Laplace derived a formula for the probability that the next trial will be a success.

$$\Pr(\text{next outcome is success}) = \frac{s+1}{n+2}$$

where s is the number of previously observed successes and n is the total number of observed trials. It is still used as an estimator for the probability of an event if we know the event space, but only have a small number of samples.

The rule of succession has been subject to much criticism, partly due to the example which Laplace chose to illustrate it. He calculated that the probability that the sun will rise tomorrow, given that it has never failed to in the past, was

$$\Pr(\text{sun will rise tomorrow}) = \frac{d+1}{d+2}$$

where d is the number of times the sun has risen in the past. This result has been derided as absurd, and some authors have concluded that all applications of the Rule of Succession are absurd by extension. However, Laplace was fully aware of the absurdity of the result; immediately following the example, he wrote, "But this number [i.e., the probability that the sun will rise tomorrow] is far greater for him who, seeing in the totality of phenomena the principle regulating the days and seasons, realizes that nothing at the present moment can arrest the course of it."[28]

Laplace's demon

Laplace strongly believed in causal determinism, which is expressed in the following quote from the introduction to the *Essai*:

> We may regard the present state of the universe as the effect of its past and the cause of its future. An intellect which at a certain moment would know all forces that set nature in motion, and all positions of all items of which nature is composed, if this intellect were also vast enough to submit these data to analysis, it would embrace in a single formula the movements of the greatest bodies of the universe and those of the tiniest atom; for such an intellect nothing would be uncertain and the future just like the past would be present before its eyes.

> —Pierre Simon Laplace, *A Philosophical Essay on Probabilities*[29]

This intellect is often referred to as *Laplace's Superman* or *Laplace's demon* (in the same vein as Maxwell's demon). Note that the description of the hypothetical intellect described above by Laplace as a demon does not come from Laplace, but from later biographers: Laplace saw himself as a scientist who hoped that humanity would progress in a better scientific understanding of the world, which, if and when eventually completed, would still need a tremendous calculating power to compute it all in a single instant.

Laplace transforms

As early as 1744, Euler, followed by Lagrange, had started looking for solutions of differential equations in the form:[30]

$$z = \int X(x)e^{ax}\, dx \text{ and } z = \int X(x)x^a\, dx.$$

In 1785, Laplace took the key forward step in using integrals of this form in order to transform a whole difference equation, rather than simply as a form for the solution, and found that the transformed equation was easier to solve than the original.[31] [32]

Other discoveries and accomplishments

Mathematics

Amongst the other discoveries of Laplace in pure and applicable mathematics are:

- Discussion, contemporaneously with Alexandre-Théophile Vandermonde, of the general theory of determinants, (1772);[6]
- Proof that every equation of an even degree must have at least one real quadratic factor;[6]
- Solution of the linear partial differential equation of the second order;[6]
- He was the first to consider the difficult problems involved in equations of mixed differences, and to prove that the solution of an equation in finite differences of the first degree and the second order might be always obtained in the form of a continued fraction;[6] and
- In his theory of probabilities:
  - Evaluation of several common definite integrals;[6] and
  - General proof of the Lagrange reversion theorem.[6]

Surface tension

Laplace built upon the qualitative work of Thomas Young to develop the theory of capillary action and the Young-Laplace equation.

Speed of sound

Laplace in 1816 was the first to point out that the speed of sound in air depends on the heat capacity ratio. Newton's original theory gave too low a value, because it does not take account of the adiabatic compression of the air which results in a local rise in temperature and pressure. Laplace's investigations in practical physics were confined to those carried on by him jointly with Lavoisier in the years 1782 to 1784 on the specific heat of various bodies.[6]

Political ambitions

According to W. W. Rouse Ball, as Napoleon's power increased Laplace begged him to give him the post of Minister of the Interior. However this is disputed by Pearson.[3] Napoleon, who desired the support of men of science, did make him Minister of the Interior in November 1799, but a little less than six weeks saw the close of Laplace's political career. Napoleon later (in his *Mémoires de Sainte Hélène*) wrote of his dismissal as follows:[6]

> Géomètre de premier rang, Laplace ne tarda pas à se montrer administrateur plus que médiocre; dès son premier travail nous reconnûmes que nous nous étions trompé. Laplace ne saisissait aucune question sous son véritable point de vue: il cherchait des subtilités partout, n'avait que des idées problématiques, et portait enfin l'esprit des `infiniment petits' jusque dans l'administration. (Geometrician of the first rank, Laplace was not long in showing himself a worse than average administrator; since his first actions in office we recognized our mistake. Laplace did not consider any question from the right angle: he sought subtleties everywhere, only conceived problems, and finally carried the spirit of "infinitesimals" into the administration.)

Laplace

Lucien, Napoleon's brother, was given the post. Although Laplace was removed from office, it was desirable to retain his allegiance. He was accordingly raised to the senate, and to the third volume of the *Mécanique céleste* he prefixed a note that of all the truths therein contained the most precious to the author was the declaration he thus made of his devotion towards the peacemaker of Europe. In copies sold after the Bourbon Restoration this was struck out. (Pearson points out that the censor would not have allowed it anyway.) In 1814 it was evident that the empire was falling; Laplace hastened to tender his services to the Bourbons, and in 1817 during the Restoration he was rewarded with the title of marquis.

According to Rouse Ball, the contempt that his more honest colleagues felt for his conduct in the matter may be read in the pages of Paul Louis Courier. His knowledge was useful on the numerous scientific commissions on which he served, and probably accounts for the manner in which his political insincerity was overlooked.[6]

He died in Paris in 1827. His brain was removed by his physician, François Magendie, and kept for many years, eventually being displayed in a roving anatomical museum in Britain. It was reportedly smaller than the average brain.[3]

Honours

- Asteroid 4628 Laplace is named for him.[33]
- He is one of only seventy-two people to have their name engraved on the Eiffel Tower.
- The European Space Agency's working-title for the international Europa Jupiter System Mission is "Laplace".

Quotes

- What we know is not much. What we do not know is immense. (attributed)
- I had no need of that hypothesis. ("Je n'avais pas besoin de cette hypothèse-là", as a reply to Napoleon, who had asked why he hadn't mentioned God in his book on astronomy.)
- "It is therefore obvious that ..." (frequently used in the *Celestial Mechanics* when he had proved something and mislaid the proof, or found it clumsy. Notorious as a signal for something true, but hard to prove.)
- The weight of evidence for an extraordinary claim must be proportioned to its strangeness.[34]
- "...(This simplicity of ratios will not appear astonishing if we consider that) all the effects of nature are only mathematical results of a small number of immutable laws." [29]

Bibliography

By Laplace

- *Œuvres complètes de Laplace* [35], 14 vol. (1878–1912), Paris: Gauthier-Villars (copy from Gallica in French)
- *Théorie du movement et de la figure elliptique des planètes* (1784) Paris (not in *Œuvres complètes*)
- *Précis de l'histoire de l'astronomie* [36]

English translations

- Bowditch, N. (trans.) (1829–1839) *Mécanique céleste*, 4 vols, Boston
  - New edition by Reprint Services ISBN 078122022X
- — [1829–1839] (1966–1969) *Celestial Mechanics*, 5 vols, including the original French
- Pound, J. (trans.) (1809) *The System of the World*, 2 vols, London: Richard Phillips
- _ *The System of the World (v.1)* [37]
- _ *The System of the World (v.2)* [38]
- — [1809] (2007) *The System of the World*, vol.1, Kessinger, ISBN 1432653679
- Toplis, J. (trans.) (1814) A treatise upon analytical mechanics [39] Nottingham: H. Barnett
- Truscott, F. W. & Emory, F. L. (trans.) (2007) [1902]. *A Philosophical Essay on Probabilities*. ISBN 1602063281., translated from the French 6th ed. (1840)
  - *A Philosophical Essay on Probabilities (1902)* [40] at the Internet Archive

About Laplace and his work

- Andoyer, H. (1922). *L'œuvre scientifique de Laplace*. Paris: Payot. (in French)
- Bigourdan, G. (1931). "La jeunesse de P.-S. Laplace" (in French). *La Science moderne* **9**: 377–384.
- Crosland, M. (1967). *The Society of Arcueil: A View of French Science at the Time of Napoleon I*. Cambridge MA: Harvard University Press. ISBN 043554201X.
- Dale, A. I. (1982). "Bayes or Laplace? an examination of the origin and early application of Bayes' theorem". *Archive for the History of the Exact Sciences* **27**: 23–47.
- David, F. N. (1965) "Some notes on Laplace", in Neyman, J. & LeCam, L. M. (eds) *Bernoulli, Bayes and Laplace*, Berlin, *pp*30–44

- Deakin, M. A. B. (1981). "The development of the Laplace transform". *Archive for the History of the Exact Sciences* **25**: 343–390. doi:10.1007/BF01395660.
- — (1982). "The development of the Laplace transform". *Archive for the History of the Exact Sciences* **26**: 351–381. doi:10.1007/BF00418754.
- Dhombres, J. (1989). "La théorie de la capillarité selon Laplace: mathématisation superficielle ou étendue" (in French). *Revue d'Histoire des sciences et de leurs applications* **62**: 43–70.
- Duveen, D. & Hahn, R. (1957). "Laplace's succession to Bezout's post of Examinateur des élèves de l'artillerie". *Isis* **48**: 416–427. doi:10.1086/348608.
- Finn, B. S. (1964). "Laplace and the speed of sound". *Isis* **55**: 7–19. doi:10.1086/349791.
- Fourier, J. B. J. (1827). "Éloge historique de M. le Marquis de Laplace". *Mémoires de l'Académie Royale des Sciences* **10**: lxxxi–cii., delivered 15 June 1829, published in 1831. (in French)
- Gillispie, C. C. (1972). "Probability and politics: Laplace, Condorcet, and Turgot". *Proceedings of the American Philosophical Society* **116(1)**: 1–20.
- — (1997) *Pierre Simon Laplace 1749–1827: A Life in Exact Science*, Princeton: Princeton University Press, ISBN 0-691-01185-0
- Grattan-Guinness, I., 2005, "'Exposition du système du monde' and 'Traité de méchanique céleste'" in his *Landmark Writings in Western Mathematics*. Elsevier: 242–57.
- Hahn, R. (1955). "Laplace's religious views". *Archives internationales d'histoire des sciences* **8**: 38–40.
- — (1982). *Calendar of the Correspondence of Pierre Simon Laplace* (Berkeley Papers in the History of Science, vol.8 ed.). Berkeley, CA: University of California.
- — (1994). *New Calendar of the Correspondence of Pierre Simon Laplace* (Berkeley Papers in the History of Science, vol.16 ed.). Berkeley, CA: University of California.
- — (2005) *Pierre Simon Laplace 1749–1827: A Determined Scientist*, Cambridge, MA: Harvard University Press, ISBN 0-674-01892-3
- Israel, Werner (1987). "Dark stars: the evolution of an idea". in Hawking, Stephen W.; Israel, Werner. *300 Years of Gravitation*. Cambridge University Press. pp. 199–276
- O'Connor, John J.; Robertson, Edmund F., "Laplace" [41], *MacTutor History of Mathematics archive*, University of St Andrews. (1999)
- Rouse Ball, W. W. [1908] (2003) "Pierre Simon Laplace (1749–1827) [42]", in *A Short Account of the History of Mathematics*, 4th ed., Dover, ISBN 0486206300
- Stigler, S. M. (1975). "Napoleonic statistics: the work of Laplace" [43]. *Biometrika* (Biometrika, Vol. 62, No. 2) **62** (2): 503–517. doi:10.2307/2335393.
- — (1978). "Laplace's early work: chronology and citations". *Isis* **69(2)**: 234–254.
- Whitrow, G. J. (2001) "Laplace, Pierre-Simon, marquis de", *Encyclopaedia Britannica*, Deluxe CDROM edition
- Whittaker, E. T. (1949a). "Laplace" [44]. *Mathematical Gazette* (The Mathematical Gazette, Vol. 33, No. 303) **33** (303): 1–12. doi:10.2307/3608408.
- — (1949b). "Laplace". *American Mathematical Monthly* **56(6)**: 369–372.
- Wilson, C. (1985). "The Great Inequality of Jupiter and Saturn: from Kepler to Laplace". *Archive for the History of the Exact Sciences* **33(1–3)**: 15–290. doi:10.1007/BF00328048.
- Young, T. (1821). *Elementary Illustrations of the Celestial Mechanics of Laplace: Part the First, Comprehending the First Book* [45]. London: John Murray. (available from Google Books)

External links

- "Laplace, Pierre (1749–1827)" [46]. *Eric Weisstein's World of Scientific Biography*. Wolfram Research. Retrieved 2007-08-24.
- "Pierre-Simon Laplace [41]" in the MacTutor History of Mathematics archive.
- "Bowditch's English translation of Laplace's preface" [47]. *Méchanique Céleste*. The MacTutor History of Mathematics archive. Retrieved 2007-09-04.
- Guide to the Pierre Simon Laplace Papers [48] at The Bancroft Library
- Laplace's math genealogy [49]
- English translation [50] of a large part of Laplace's work in probability and statistics, provided by Richard Pulskamp [51]

References

[1] Stephen M. Stigler (1986) The history of statistics. Harvard University press. Chapter 3.
[2] [Anon.] (1911) " Pierre Simon, Marquis De Laplace (http://www.1911encyclopedia.org/Pierre_Simon,_Marquis_De_Laplace)", *Encyclopaedia Britannica*
[3] "Laplace, being Extracts from Lectures delivered by Karl Pearson", *Biometrika*, vol. 21, Dec. 1929, pp. 202–16
[4] *O'Connor, John J.; Robertson, Edmund F., "Laplace" (http://www-history.mcs.st-andrews.ac.uk/Biographies/Laplace.html), *MacTutor History of Mathematics archive*, University of St Andrews, ., accessed 25 August 2007
[5] Gillispie (1997) *pp*3–4
[6] Rouse Ball (1908)
[7] Gillispie (1997) *pp*5
[8] |(1913). "Pierre-Simon Laplace" (http://en.wikipedia.org/wiki/Wikisource:catholic_encyclopedia_(1913)/pierre-simon_laplace). *Catholic Encyclopedia*. New York: Robert Appleton Company. .
[9] Gillispie (1989) *pp*7–12
[10] Gillispie (1989) *pp*14–15
[11] Whitrow (2001)
[12] Celletti, A. & Perozzi, E. (2007). *Celestial Mechanics: The Waltz of the Planets*. Berlin: Springer. pp. 91–93. ISBN 0-387-30777-X.
[13] Whittaker (1949b)
[14] Gillispie (1989) *pp*29–35
[15] Gillispie (1989) *pp*35–36
[16] School of Mathematics and Statistics (http://www-history.mcs.st-andrews.ac.uk/Biographies/Laplace.html), University of St Andrews, Scotland.
[17] Grattan-Guinness, I. (2003). *Companion Encyclopedia of the History and Philosophy of the Mathematical Sciences* (http://books.google.com/?id=f5FqsDPVQ2MC&pg=PA1098&lpg=PA1098&dq=laplace+potential+1784). Baltimore: Johns Hopkins University Press. pp. 1097–1098. ISBN 0801873967. .
[18] E Halley (1695), "Some Account of the Ancient State of the City of Palmyra, with Short Remarks upon the Inscriptions Found there" (http://rstl.royalsocietypublishing.org/content/19/215-235/160.full.pdf), *Phil. Trans.*, vol.19 (1695-1697), pages 160-175; esp. at pages 174-175.
[19] Richard Dunthorne (1749), "A Letter from the Rev. Mr. Richard Dunthorne to the Reverend Mr. Richard Mason F. R. S. and Keeper of the Wood-Wardian Museum at Cambridge, concerning the Acceleration of the Moon" (http://rstl.royalsocietypublishing.org/content/46/491-496/162.full.pdf), *Philosophical Transactions (1683-1775)*, Vol. 46 (1749 - 1750) #492, pp.162-172; also given in Philosophical Transactions (abridgements) (1809), vol.9 (for 1744-49), p669-675 (http://www.archive.org/stream/philosophicaltra09royarich#page/669/mode/2up) as "On the Acceleration of the Moon, by the Rev. Richard Dunthorne".
[20] J de Lalande (1786): "Sur les equations seculaires du soleil et de la lune" (http://www.academie-sciences.fr/membres/in_memoriam/Lalande/Lalande_pdf/Mem1786_p390.pdf), Memoires de l'Academie Royale des Sciences, pp.390-397, at page 395.
[21] J D North (2008), "Cosmos: an illustrated history of astronomy and cosmology", (University of Chicago Press, 2008), chapter 14, at page 454 (http://books.google.com/books?id=qq8Luhs7rTUC&pg=PA454).
[22] See also P Puiseux (1879), "Sur l'acceleration seculaire du mouvement de la Lune" (http://archive.numdam.org/article/ASENS_1879_2_8__361_0.pdf), Annales Scientifiques de l'Ecole Normale Superieure, 2nd series vol.8 (1879), pp.361-444, at pages 361-5.
[23] J C Adams (1853), "On the Secular Variation of the Moon's Mean Motion" (http://rstl.royalsocietypublishing.org/content/143/397.full.pdf), in *Phil. Trans. R. Soc. Lond.*, vol.143 (1853), pages 397-406.
[24] Roy, A. E. (2005). *Orbital Motion* (http://books.google.com/?id=Hzv7k2vH6PgC&pg=PA313&lpg=PA313&dq=laplace+secular+acceleration). London: CRC Press. pp. 313. ISBN 0750310154. .
[25] Owen, T. C. (2001) "Solar system: origin of the solar system", *Encyclopaedia Britannica*, Deluxe CDROM edition
[26] Crosland (1967) *p.*1

[27] See Israel (1987), sec. 7.2.

[28] Laplace, Pierre Simon, *A Philosophical Essay on Probabilities*, translated from the 6th French edition by Frederick Wilson Truscott and Frederick Lincoln Emory, Dover Publications (New York, 1951)

[29] Laplace, Pierre Simon, *A Philosophical Essay on Probabilities*, translated from the 6th French edition by Frederick Wilson Truscott and Frederick Lincoln Emory, Dover Publications (New York, 1951) pp.4

[30] Grattan-Guiness, in Gillispie (1997) *p.260*

[31] Grattan-Guiness, in Gillispie (1997) *pp261–262*

[32] Deakin (1981)

[33] Schmadel, L. D. (2003). *Dictionary of Minor Planet Names* (5th rev. ed.). Berlin: Springer-Verlag. ISBN 3540002383.

[34] A sense of place in the heartland (http://www.jsonline.com/story/index.aspx?id=497783&format=print), The Milwaukee Journal Sentinel Online

C++

The C++ Programming Language, written by its architect, is the seminal book on the language.

Paradigm	Multi-paradigm:[1] procedural, object-oriented, generic
Appeared in	1983
Designed by	Bjarne Stroustrup
Developer	Bjarne Stroustrup Bell Labs ISO/IEC JTC1/SC22/WG21
Stable release	ISO/IEC 14882:2003 (2003)
Preview release	C++0x
Typing discipline	Static, unsafe, nominative
Major implementations	Borland C++ Builder, GCC, Intel C++ Compiler, Microsoft Visual C++, Sun Studio, Turbo C++, Comeau C/C++, clang
Dialects	ISO/IEC C++ 1998, ISO/IEC C++ 2003
Influenced by	C, Simula, Ada 83, ALGOL 68, CLU, ML[1]
Influenced	Perl, LPC, Lua, Pike, Ada 95, Java, PHP, D, C99, C#, Aikido, Falcon
OS	Cross-platform (multi-platform)
Usual file extensions	.h .hh .hpp .hxx .h++ .cc .cpp .cxx .c++
⅀ C++ Programming at Wikibooks	

C++ (pronounced *see plus plus*) is a statically typed, free-form, multi-paradigm, compiled, general-purpose programming language. It is regarded as a "middle-level" language, as it comprises a combination of both high-level and low-level language features.[2] It was developed by Bjarne Stroustrup starting in 1979 at Bell Labs as an enhancement to the C programming language and originally named *C with Classes*. It was renamed *C++* in 1983.[3]

As one of the most popular programming languages ever created,[4] [5] C++ is widely used in the software industry. Some of its application domains include systems software, application software, device drivers, embedded software, high-performance server and client applications, and entertainment software such as video games. Several groups provide both free and proprietary C++ compiler software, including the GNU Project, Microsoft, Intel and Borland. C++ has greatly influenced many other popular programming languages, most notably Java.

C++ is also used for hardware design, where design is initially described in C++, then analyzed, architecturally constrained, and scheduled to create a register transfer level hardware description language via high-level synthesis.

The language began as enhancements to C, first adding classes, then virtual functions, operator overloading, multiple inheritance, templates, and exception handling among other features. After years of development, the C++ programming language standard was ratified in 1998 as *ISO/IEC 14882:1998*. That standard is still current, but is amended by the 2003 technical corrigendum, *ISO/IEC 14882:2003*. The next standard version (known informally as

C++0x) is in development.

History

Bjarne Stroustrup began work on "C with Classes" in 1979. The idea of creating a new language originated from Stroustrup's experience in programming for his Ph.D. thesis. Stroustrup found that Simula had features that were very helpful for large software development, but the language was too slow for practical use, while BCPL was fast but too low-level to be suitable for large software development. When Stroustrup started working in AT&T Bell Labs, he had the problem of analyzing the UNIX kernel with respect to distributed computing. Remembering his Ph.D. experience, Stroustrup set out to enhance the C language with Simula-like features. C was chosen because it was general-purpose, fast, portable and widely used. Besides C and Simula,

Bjarne Stroustrup, creator of C++

some other languages that inspired him were ALGOL 68, Ada, CLU and ML. At first, the class, derived class, strong type checking, inlining, and default argument features were added to C via Stroustrup's C++ to C compiler, Cfront. The first commercial implementation of C++ was released in October 1985.[6]

In 1983, the name of the language was changed from *C with Classes* to C++ (++ being the increment operator in C). New features were added including virtual functions, function name and operator overloading, references, constants, user-controlled free-store memory control, improved type checking, and BCPL style single-line comments with two forward slashes (//). In 1985, the first edition of *The C++ Programming Language* was released, providing an important reference to the language, since there was not yet an official standard. Release 2.0 of C++ came in 1989. New features included multiple inheritance, abstract classes, static member functions, const member functions, and protected members. In 1990, *The Annotated C++ Reference Manual* was published. This work became the basis for the future standard. Late addition of features included templates, exceptions, namespaces, new casts, and a Boolean type.

As the C++ language evolved, the standard library evolved with it. The first addition to the C++ standard library was the stream I/O library which provided facilities to replace the traditional C functions such as printf and scanf. Later, among the most significant additions to the standard library, was the Standard Template Library.

C++ continues to be used and is one of the preferred programming languages to develop professional applications. The popularity of the language continues to grow.[7]

Language standard

In 1998, the C++ standards committee (the ISO/IEC JTC1/SC22/WG21 working group) standardized C++ and published the international standard *ISO/IEC 14882:1998* (informally known as *C++98*[8]). For some years after the official release of the standard, the committee processed defect reports, and published a corrected version of the C++ standard, *ISO/IEC 14882:2003*, in 2003. In 2005, a technical report, called the "Library Technical Report 1" (often known as TR1 for short), was released. While not an official part of the standard, it specified a number of extensions to the standard library, which were expected to be included in the next version of C++. Support for TR1 is growing in almost all currently maintained C++ compilers.

The standard for the next version of the language (known informally as C++0x) is in development.

Etymology

According to Stroustrup: "the name signifies the evolutionary nature of the changes from C".[9] During C++'s development period, the language had been referred to as "new C", then "C with Classes". The final name is credited to Rick Mascitti (mid-1983) and was first used in December 1983. When Mascitti was questioned informally in 1992 about the naming, he indicated that it was given in a tongue-in-cheek spirit. It stems from C's "++" operator (which increments the value of a variable) and a common naming convention of using "+" to indicate an enhanced computer program. There is no language called "C plus". ABCL/c+ was the name of an earlier, unrelated programming language.

Philosophy

In *The Design and Evolution of C++* (1994), Bjarne Stroustrup describes some rules that he used for the design of C++:

- C++ is designed to be a statically typed, general-purpose language that is as efficient and portable as C
- C++ is designed to directly and comprehensively support multiple programming styles (procedural programming, data abstraction, object-oriented programming, and generic programming)
- C++ is designed to give the programmer choice, even if this makes it possible for the programmer to choose incorrectly
- C++ is designed to be as compatible with C as possible, therefore providing a smooth transition from C
- C++ avoids features that are platform specific or not general purpose
- C++ does not incur overhead for features that are not used (the "zero-overhead principle")
- C++ is designed to function without a sophisticated programming environment

Stroustrup also mentions that C++ was always intended to make programming more *fun* and that many of the double meanings in the language are intentional.

Inside the C++ Object Model (Lippman, 1996) describes how compilers may convert C++ program statements into an in-memory layout. Compiler authors are, however, free to implement the standard in their own manner.

Standard library

The 1998 ANSI/ISO C++ standard consists of two parts: the core language and the C++ Standard Library; the latter includes most of the Standard Template Library (STL) and a slightly modified version of the C standard library. Many C++ libraries exist which are not part of the standard, and, using linkage specification, libraries can even be written in languages such as C, Fortran, Pascal, or BASIC. Which of these are supported is compiler dependent.

The C++ standard library incorporates the C standard library with some small modifications to make it optimized with the C++ language. Another large part of the C++ library is based on the STL. This provides such useful tools as containers (for example vectors and lists), iterators to provide these containers with array-like access and algorithms to perform operations such as searching and sorting. Furthermore (multi)maps (associative arrays) and (multi)sets are provided, all of which export compatible interfaces. Therefore it is possible, using templates, to write generic algorithms that work with any container or on any sequence defined by iterators. As in C, the features of the library are accessed by using the #include directive to include a standard header. C++ provides 69 standard headers, of which 19 are deprecated.

The STL was originally a third-party library from HP and later SGI, before its incorporation into the C++ standard. The standard does not refer to it as "STL", as it is merely a part of the standard library, but many people still use that term to distinguish it from the rest of the library (input/output streams, internationalization, diagnostics, the C library subset, etc.).

Most C++ compilers provide an implementation of the C++ standard library, including the STL. Compiler-independent implementations of the STL, such as STLPort,[10] also exist. Other projects also produce various custom implementations of the C++ standard library and the STL with various design goals.

Language features

C++ inherits most of C's syntax. The following is Bjarne Stroustrup's version of the Hello world program which uses the C++ standard library stream facility to write a message to standard output:[11] [12]

```
#include <iostream>

int main()
{
    std::cout << "Hello, world!\n";
}
```

Within functions that define a non-void return type, failure to return a value before control reaches the end of the function results in undefined behaviour (compilers typically provide the means to issue a diagnostic in such a case).[13] The sole exception to this rule is the main function, which implicitly returns a value of zero.[14]

Operators and operator overloading

C++ provides more than 30 operators, covering basic arithmetic, bit manipulation, indirection, comparisons, logical operations and others. Almost all operators can be overloaded for user-defined types, with a few notable exceptions such as member access (. and .*). The rich set of overloadable operators is central to using C++ as a domain specific language. The overloadable operators are also an essential part of many advanced C++ programming techniques, such as smart pointers. Overloading an operator does not change the precedence of calculations involving the operator, nor does it change the number of operands that the operator uses (any operand may however be ignored by the operator, though it will be evaluated prior to execution). Overloaded "&&" and "||" operators lose their short-circuit evaluation property.

Templates

C++ templates enable generic programming. C++ supports both function and class templates. Templates may be parameterized by types, compile-time constants, and other templates. C++ templates are implemented by *instantiation* at compile-time. To instantiate a template, compilers substitute specific arguments for a template's parameters to generate a concrete function or class instance. Some substitutions are not possible; these are eliminated by an overload resolution policy described by the phrase "Substitution failure is not an error" (SFINAE). Templates are a powerful tool that can be used for generic programming, template metaprogramming, and code optimization, but this power implies a cost. Template use may increase code size, since each template instantiation produces a copy of the template code: one for each set of template arguments. This is in contrast to run-time generics seen in other languages (e.g. Java) where at compile-time the type is erased and a single template body is preserved.

Templates are different from macros: while both of these compile-time language features enable conditional compilation, templates are not restricted to lexical substitution. Templates are aware of the semantics and type system of their companion language, as well as all compile-time type definitions, and can perform high-level operations including programmatic flow control based on evaluation of strictly type-checked parameters. Macros are capable of conditional control over compilation based on predetermined criteria, but cannot instantiate new types, recurse, or perform type evaluation and in effect are limited to pre-compilation text-substitution and text-inclusion/exclusion. In other words, macros can control compilation flow based on pre-defined symbols but cannot, unlike templates, independently instantiate new symbols. Templates are a tool for static polymorphism (see below) and generic programming.

In addition, templates are a compile time mechanism in C++ which is Turing-complete, meaning that any computation expressible by a computer program can be computed, in some form, by a template metaprogram prior to runtime.

In summary, a template is a compile-time parameterized function or class written without knowledge of the specific arguments used to instantiate it. After instantiation the resulting code is equivalent to code written specifically for the passed arguments. In this manner, templates provide a way to decouple generic, broadly applicable aspects of functions and classes (encoded in templates) from specific aspects (encoded in template parameters) without sacrificing performance due to abstraction.

Objects

C++ introduces object-oriented (OO) features to C. It offers classes, which provide the four features commonly present in OO (and some non-OO) languages: abstraction, encapsulation, inheritance, and polymorphism. Objects are instances of classes created at runtime. The class can be thought of as a template from which many different individual objects may be generated as a program runs.

Encapsulation

Encapsulation is the hiding of information in order to ensure that data structures and operators are used as intended and to make the usage model more obvious to the developer. C++ provides the ability to define classes and functions as its primary encapsulation mechanisms. Within a class, members can be declared as either public, protected, or private in order to explicitly enforce encapsulation. A public member of the class is accessible to any function. A private member is accessible only to functions that are members of that class and to functions and classes explicitly granted access permission by the class ("friends"). A protected member is accessible to members of classes that inherit from the class in addition to the class itself and any friends.

The OO principle is that all of the functions (and only the functions) that access the internal representation of a type should be encapsulated within the type definition. C++ supports this (via member functions and friend functions), but does not enforce it: the programmer can declare parts or all of the representation of a type to be public, and is allowed to make public entities that are not part of the representation of the type. Because of this, C++ supports not just OO programming, but other weaker decomposition paradigms, like modular programming.

It is generally considered good practice to make all data private or protected, and to make public only those functions that are part of a minimal interface for users of the class. This hides all the details of data implementation, allowing the designer to later fundamentally change the implementation without changing the interface in any way.[15] [16]

Inheritance

Inheritance allows one data type to acquire properties of other data types. Inheritance from a base class may be declared as public, protected, or private. This access specifier determines whether unrelated and derived classes can access the inherited public and protected members of the base class. Only public inheritance corresponds to what is usually meant by "inheritance". The other two forms are much less frequently used. If the access specifier is omitted, a "class" inherits privately, while a "struct" inherits publicly. Base classes may be declared as virtual; this is called virtual inheritance. Virtual inheritance ensures that only one instance of a base class exists in the inheritance graph, avoiding some of the ambiguity problems of multiple inheritance.

Multiple inheritance is a C++ feature not found in most other languages. Multiple inheritance allows a class to be derived from more than one base class; this allows for more elaborate inheritance relationships. For example, a "Flying Cat" class can inherit from both "Cat" and "Flying Mammal". Some other languages, such as Java or C#, accomplish something similar (although more limited) by allowing inheritance of multiple interfaces while restricting the number of base classes to one (interfaces, unlike classes, provide only declarations of member functions, no implementation or member data). An interface as in Java and C# can be defined in C++ as a class containing only pure virtual functions, often known as an abstract base class or "ABC". The member functions of such an abstract base classes are normally explicitly defined in the derived class, not inherited implicitly.

Polymorphism

Polymorphism enables one common interface for many implementations, and for objects to act differently under different circumstances.

C++ supports several kinds of *static* (compile-time) and *dynamic* (run-time) polymorphisms. Compile-time polymorphism does not allow for certain run-time decisions, while run-time polymorphism typically incurs a performance penalty.

Static polymorphism

Function overloading allows programs to declare multiple functions having the same name (but with different arguments). The functions are distinguished by the number and/or types of their formal parameters. Thus, the same function name can refer to different functions depending on the context in which it is used. The type returned by the function is not used to distinguish overloaded functions.

When declaring a function, a programmer can specify default value for one or more parameters. Doing so allows the parameters with defaults to optionally be omitted when the function is called, in which case the default arguments will be used. When a function is called with fewer arguments than there are declared parameters, explicit arguments are matched to parameters in left-to-right order, with any unmatched parameters at the end of the parameter list being assigned their default arguments. In many cases, specifying default arguments in a single function declaration is preferable to providing overloaded function definitions with different numbers of parameters.

Templates in C++ provide a sophisticated mechanism for writing generic, polymorphic code. In particular, through the Curiously Recurring Template Pattern it's possible to implement a form of static polymorphism that closely mimics the syntax for overriding virtual functions. Since C++ templates are type-aware and Turing-complete they can also be used to let the compiler resolve recursive conditionals and generate substantial programs through template metaprogramming.

Dynamic polymorphism

Inheritance

Variable pointers (and references) to a base class type in C++ can refer to objects of any derived classes of that type in addition to objects exactly matching the variable type. This allows arrays and other kinds of containers to hold pointers to objects of differing types. Because assignment of values to variables usually occurs at run-time, this is necessarily a run-time phenomenon.

C++ also provides a dynamic_cast operator, which allows the program to safely attempt conversion of an object into an object of a more specific object type (as opposed to conversion to a more general type, which is always allowed). This feature relies on run-time type information (RTTI). Objects known to be of a certain specific type can also be cast to that type with static_cast, a purely compile-time construct which is faster and does not require RTTI.

Virtual member functions

Ordinarily when a function in a derived class overrides a function in a base class, the function to call is determined by the type of the object. A given function is overridden when there exists no difference, in the number or type of parameters, between two or more definitions of that function. Hence, at compile time it may not be possible to determine the type of the object and therefore the correct function to call, given only a base class pointer; the decision is therefore put off until runtime. This is called dynamic dispatch. Virtual member functions or *methods*[17] allow the most specific implementation of the function to be called, according to the actual run-time type of the object. In C++ implementations, this is commonly done using virtual function tables. If the object type is known, this may be bypassed by prepending a fully qualified class name before the function call, but in general calls to virtual functions are resolved at run time.

In addition to standard member functions, operator overloads and destructors can be virtual. A general rule of thumb is that if any functions in the class are virtual, the destructor should be as well. As the type of an object at its creation is known at compile time, constructors, and by extension copy constructors, cannot be virtual. Nonetheless a situation may arise where a copy of an object needs to be created when a pointer to a derived object is passed as a pointer to a base object. In such a case a common solution is to create a clone() (or similar) function and declare that as virtual. The clone() method creates and returns a copy of the derived class when called.

A member function can also be made "pure virtual" by appending it with = 0 after the closing parenthesis and before the semicolon. Objects cannot be created of a class with a pure virtual function and are called abstract data types. Such abstract data types can only be derived from. Any derived class inherits the virtual function as pure and must provide a non-pure definition of it (and all other pure virtual functions) before objects of the derived class can be created. A program that attempts to create an object of a class with a pure virtual member function or inherited pure virtual member function is ill-formed.

Parsing and processing C++ source code

It is relatively difficult to write a good C++ parser with classic parsing algorithms such as LALR(1).[18] This is partly because the C++ grammar is not LALR. Because of this, there are very few tools for analyzing or performing non-trivial transformations (e.g., refactoring) of existing code. One way to handle this difficulty is to choose a different syntax, such as Significantly Prettier and Easier C++ Syntax, which is LALR(1) parsable. More powerful parsers, such as GLR parsers, can be substantially simpler (though slower).

Parsing (in the literal sense of producing a syntax tree) is not the most difficult problem in building a C++ processing tool. Such tools must also have the same understanding of the meaning of the identifiers in the program as a compiler might have. Practical systems for processing C++ must then not only parse the source text, but be able to resolve for each identifier precisely which definition applies (e.g. they must correctly handle C++'s complex scoping rules) and what its type is, as well as the types of larger expressions.

Finally, a practical C++ processing tool must be able to handle the variety of C++ dialects used in practice (such as that supported by the GNU Compiler Collection and that of Microsoft's Visual C++) and implement appropriate analyzers, source code transformers, and regenerate source text. Combining advanced parsing algorithms such as GLR with symbol table construction and program transformation machinery can enable the construction of arbitrary C++ tools.

Compatibility

Producing a reasonably standards-compliant C++ compiler has proven to be a difficult task for compiler vendors in general. For many years, different C++ compilers implemented the C++ language to different levels of compliance to the standard, and their implementations varied widely in some areas such as partial template specialization. Recent releases of most popular C++ compilers support almost all of the C++ 1998 standard.[19]

In order to give compiler vendors greater freedom, the C++ standards committee decided not to dictate the implementation of name mangling, exception handling, and other implementation-specific features. The downside of this decision is that object code produced by different compilers is expected to be incompatible. There are, however, third party standards for particular machines or operating systems which attempt to standardize compilers on those platforms (for example C++ ABI[20]); some compilers adopt a secondary standard for these items.

With C

C++ is often considered to be a superset of C, but this is not strictly true.[21] Most C code can easily be made to compile correctly in C++, but there are a few differences that cause some valid C code to be invalid in C++, or to behave differently in C++.

One commonly encountered difference is that C allows implicit conversion from void* to other pointer types, but C++ does not. Another common portability issue is that C++ defines many new keywords, such as new and class, that may be used as identifiers (e.g. variable names) in a C program.

Some incompatibilities have been removed by the latest (C99) C standard, which now supports C++ features such as // comments and mixed declarations and code. On the other hand, C99 introduced a number of new features that C++ does not support, such as variable-length arrays, native complex-number types, designated initializers and compound literals.[22] However, at least some of the new C99 features will likely be included in the next version of the C++ standard, C++0x.

In order to intermix C and C++ code, any function declaration or definition that is to be called from/used both in C and C++ must be declared with C linkage by placing it within an extern "C" {/*...*/} block. Such a function may not rely on features depending on name mangling (i.e., function overloading).

Criticism

Critics of the language raise several points. First, since C++ includes C as a subset, it inherits many of the criticisms leveled at C. For its large feature set, it is criticized as being over-complicated, and difficult to fully master.[23] Bjarne Stroustrup points out that resultant executables do not support these claims of bloat: "*I have even seen the C++ version of the 'hello world' program smaller than the C version.*"[24] An Embedded C++ standard was proposed to deal with part of this, but criticized for leaving out useful parts of the language that incur no runtime penalty.[25]

Other criticism stems from what is missing from C++. For example, the current version of Standard C++ provides no language features to create multi-threaded software. These facilities are present in some other languages including Java, Ada, and C# (see also Lock). It is possible to use operating system calls or third party libraries to do multi-threaded programming, but both approaches may create portability concerns. The new C++0x standard addresses this matter by extending the language with threading facilities.

C++ is also sometimes compared unfavorably with languages such as Smalltalk, Java, or Eiffel on the basis that it enables programmers to "mix and match" object-oriented programming, procedural programming, generic programming, functional programming, declarative programming, and others, rather than strictly enforcing a single style, although C++ is intentionally a multi-paradigm language.[1]

A fraudulent article was written wherein Bjarne Stroustrup is supposedly interviewed for a 1998 issue of IEEE's 'Computer' magazine[26]. In this article, the interviewer expects to discuss the successes of C++ now that several years had passed after its introduction. Instead, Stroustrup proceeds to confess that his invention of C++ was intended to create the most complex and difficult language possible to weed out amateur programmers and raise the salaries of the few programmers who could master the language. The article contains various criticisms of C++'s complexity and poor usability, most false or exaggerated. In reality, Stroustrup wrote no such article, and due to the pervasiveness of the hoax, was compelled to publish an official denial on his website.[27].

C++ is commonly criticized for lacking built in garbage collection. On his website, Stroustrup explains that automated memory management is routinely implemented directly in C++, without need for a built-in collector, using "smart pointer" classes.[28] Garbage collection not based on reference counting is possible in C++ through external libraries.[29]

See also

- *The C++ Programming Language*
- C++0x, the planned new standard for C++
- Comparison of integrated development environments for C/C++
- Comparison of programming languages
- List of C++ compilers
- List of C++ template libraries
- Comparison of Java and C++

Further reading

- Abrahams, David; Aleksey Gurtovoy. *C++ Template Metaprogramming: Concepts, Tools, and Techniques from Boost and Beyond.* Addison-Wesley. ISBN 0-321-22725-5.
- Alexandrescu, Andrei (2001). *Modern C++ Design: Generic Programming and Design Patterns Applied.* Addison-Wesley. ISBN 0-201-70431-5.
- Alexandrescu, Andrei; Herb Sutter (2004). *C++ Design and Coding Standards: Rules and Guidelines for Writing Programs.* Addison-Wesley. ISBN 0-321-11358-6.
- Becker, Pete (2006). *The C++ Standard Library Extensions : A Tutorial and Reference.* Addison-Wesley. ISBN 0-321-41299-0.
- Brokken, Frank (2010). *C++ Annotations* [30]. University of Groningen. ISBN 90 367 0470 7.
- Coplien, James O. (1992, reprinted with corrections 1994). *Advanced C++: Programming Styles and Idioms.* ISBN 0-201-54855-0.
- Dewhurst, Stephen C. (2005). *C++ Common Knowledge: Essential Intermediate Programming.* Addison-Wesley. ISBN 0-321-32192-8.
- Information Technology Industry Council (15 October 2003). *Programming languages — C++* (Second edition ed.). Geneva: ISO/IEC. 14882:2003(E).
- Josuttis, Nicolai M. *The C++ Standard Library.* Addison-Wesley. ISBN 0-201-37926-0.
- Koenig, Andrew; Barbara E. Moo (2000). *Accelerated C++ - Practical Programming by Example.* Addison-Wesley. ISBN 0-201-70353-X.
- Lippman, Stanley B.; Josée Lajoie, Barbara E. Moo (2005). *C++ Primer.* Addison-Wesley. ISBN 0-201-72148-1.
- Lippman, Stanley B. (1996). *Inside the C++ Object Model.* Addison-Wesley. ISBN 0-201-83454-5.
- Stroustrup, Bjarne (2000). *The C++ Programming Language* (Special Edition ed.). Addison-Wesley. ISBN 0-201-70073-5.
- Stroustrup, Bjarne (1994). *The Design and Evolution of C++.* Addison-Wesley. ISBN 0-201-54330-3.
- Stroustrup, Bjarne. *Programming Principles and Practice Using C++.* Addison-Wesley. ISBN 0321543726.
- Sutter, Herb (2001). *More Exceptional C++: 40 New Engineering Puzzles, Programming Problems, and Solutions.* Addison-Wesley. ISBN 0-201-70434-X.
- Sutter, Herb (2004). *Exceptional C++ Style.* Addison-Wesley. ISBN 0-201-76042-8.
- Vandevoorde, David; Nicolai M. Josuttis (2003). *C++ Templates: The complete Guide.* Addison-Wesley. ISBN 0-201-73484-2.
- Scott Meyers (2005). *Effective C++.* Third Edition. Addison-Wesley. ISBN 0-321-33487-6

External links

- JTC1/SC22/WG21 [31] - The ISO/IEC C++ Standard Working Group
  - n3092.pdf [32] - Final Committee Draft of "ISO/IEC IS 14882 - Programming Languages - C++" (26 March 2010)
- A paper by Stroustrup showing the timeline of C++ evolution (1979-1991) [33]
- Bjarne Stroustrup's C++ Style and Technique FAQ [34]
- C++ FAQ Lite by Marshall Cline [35]
- Computer World interview with Bjarne Stroustrup [36]
- CrazyEngineers.com interview with Bjarne Stroustrup [37]
- The State of the Language: An Interview with Bjarne Stroustrup (August 15, 2008) [38]
- Code practices for not breaking binary compatibility between releases of C++ libraries [39] (from KDE Techbase)

References

[1] Stroustrup, Bjarne (1997). "1". *The C++ Programming Language* (Third ed.). ISBN 0201889544. OCLC 59193992.

[2] C++ The Complete Reference Third Edition, Herbert Schildt, Publisher: Osborne McGraw-Hill.

[3] ATT.com (http://www2.research.att.com/~bs_faq.html#invention)

[4] "Programming Language Popularity" (http://www.langpop.com/). 2009. . Retrieved 2009-01-16.

[5] "TIOBE Programming Community Index" (http://www.tiobe.com/index.php/content/paperinfo/tpci/index.html). 2009. . Retrieved 2009-05-06.

[6] "Bjarne Stroustrup's FAQ — When was C++ invented?" (http://public.research.att.com/~bs/bs_faq.html#invention). . Retrieved 30 May 2006.

[7] "Trends on C++ Programmers, Developers & Engineers" (http://www.odesk.com/trends/c++). . Retrieved 1 December 2008.

[8] Stroustrup, Bjarne. "C++ Glossary" (http://www.research.att.com/~bs/glossary.html). . Retrieved 8 June 2007.

[9] "Bjarne Stroustrup's FAQ — Where did the name "C++" come from?" (http://public.research.att.com/~bs/bs_faq.html#name). . Retrieved 16 January 2008.

[10] STLPort home page (http://www.stlport.org/), quote from "The C++ Standard Library" by Nicolai M. Josuttis, p138., ISBN 0-201 37926-0, Addison-Wesley, 1999: "An exemplary version of STL is the STLport, which is available for free for any platform"

[11] Stroustrup, Bjarne (2000). *The C++ Programming Language* (Special Edition ed.). Addison-Wesley. p. 46. ISBN 0-201-70073-5.

[12] Open issues for The C++ Programming Language (3rd Edition) (http://www.research.att.com/~bs/3rd_issues.html) - This code is copied directly from Bjarne Stroustrup's errata page (p. 633). He addresses the use of '\n' rather than std::endl. Also see www.research.att.com (http://www.research.att.com/~bs/bs_faq2.html#void-main) for an explanation of the implicit return 0; in the main function. This implicit return is *not* available in other functions.

[13] ISO/IEC (2003). *ISO/IEC 14882:2003(E): Programming Languages - C++ §6.6.3 The return statement [stmt.return]* para. 2

[14] ISO/IEC (2003). *ISO/IEC 14882:2003(E): Programming Languages - C++ §3.6.1 Main function [basic.start.main]* para. 5

[15] Sutter, Herb; Alexandrescu, Andrei (2004). *C++ Coding Standards: 101 Rules, Guidelines, and Best Practices*. Addison-Wesley.

[16] Henricson, Mats; Nyquist, Erik (1997). *Industrial Strength C++*. Prentice Hall. ISBN ISBN 0-13-120965-5.

[17] Stroustrup, Bjarne (2000). *The C++ Programming Language* (Special Edition ed.). Addison-Wesley. p. 310. ISBN 0-201-70073-5. "A virtual member function is sometimes called a *method*."

[18] Andrew Birkett. "Parsing C++ at nobugs.org" (http://www.nobugs.org/developer/parsingcpp/). Nobugs.org. . Retrieved 3 July 2009.

[19] Herb Sutter (15 April 2003). "C++ Conformance Roundup" (http://www.ddj.com/dept/cpp/184401381). *Dr. Dobb's Journal*. . Retrieved 30 May 2006.

[20] "C++ ABI" (http://www.codesourcery.com/cxx-abi/). . Retrieved 30 May 2006.

[21] "Bjarne Stroustrup's FAQ - Is C a subset of C++?" (http://public.research.att.com/~bs/bs_faq.html#C-is-subset). . Retrieved 18 January 2008.

[22] "C9X -- The New C Standard" (http://home.datacomm.ch/t_wolf/tw/c/c9x_changes.html). . Retrieved 27 December 2008.

[23] Morris, Richard (July 2, 2009). "Niklaus Wirth: Geek of the Week" (http://www.simple-talk.com/opinion/geek-of-the-week/niklaus-wirth-geek-of-the-week/). . Retrieved 8 August 2009. "C++ is a language that was designed to cater to everybody's perceived needs. As a result, the language and even more so its implementations have become complex and bulky, difficult to understand, and likely to contain errors for ever."

[24] Why is the code generated for the "Hello world" program ten times larger for C++ than for C? (http://www.research.att.com/~bs/bs_faq.html#Hello-world)

[25] What do you think of EC++? (http://www.research.att.com/~bs/bs_faq.html#EC++)

[26] Unattributed. Previously unpublished interview with Bjarne Stroustroup, designer of C++ (http://flinflon.brandonu.ca/dueck/1997/62285/stroustroup.html).

[27] Stroustrup, Bjarne. Stroustrup FAQ: Did you really give an interview to IEEE? (http://www2.research.att.com/~bs/bs_faq.html#IEEE)

[28] http://www2.research.att.com/~bs/bs_faq.html.

[29] http://www.hpl.hp.com/personal/Hans_Boehm/gc/

SPICE

SPICE (Simulation Program with Integrated Circuit Emphasis)[1] [2] is a general-purpose open source analog electronic circuit simulator. It is a powerful program that is used in IC and board-level design to check the integrity of circuit designs and to predict circuit behavior.

Introduction

Integrated circuits, unlike board-level designs composed of discrete parts, are impossible to breadboard before manufacture. Further, the high costs of photolithographic masks and other manufacturing prerequisites make it essential to design the circuit to be as close to perfect as possible before the integrated circuit is first built. Simulating the circuit with SPICE is the industry-standard way to verify circuit operation at the transistor level before committing to manufacturing an integrated circuit.

Board-level circuit designs can often be breadboarded for testing. Even with a breadboard, some circuit properties may not be accurate compared to the final printed wiring board, such as parasitic resistances and capacitances. These parasitic components can often be estimated more accurately using SPICE simulation. Also, designers may want more information about the circuit than is available from a single mock-up. For instance, circuit performance is affected by component manufacturing tolerances. In these cases it is common to use SPICE to perform Monte Carlo simulations of the effect of component variations on performance, a task which is impractical using calculations by hand for a circuit of any appreciable complexity.

Circuit simulation programs, of which SPICE and derivatives are the most prominent, take a text netlist describing the circuit elements (transistors, resistors, capacitors, etc.) and their connections, and translate[3] this description into equations to be solved. The general equations produced are nonlinear differential algebraic equations which are solved using implicit integration methods, Newton's method and sparse matrix techniques.

Origins

SPICE was developed at the Electronics Research Laboratory of the University of California, Berkeley by Laurence Nagel with direction from his research advisor, Prof. Donald Pederson. SPICE1 was largely a derivative of the CANCER program,[4] which Nagel had worked on under Prof. Ronald Rohrer. CANCER was an acronym for "Computer Analysis of Nonlinear Circuits, Excluding Radiation," a hint to Berkeley's liberalism of 1960s: at these times many circuit simulators were developed under the United States Department of Defense contracts that required the capability to evaluate the radiation hardness of a circuit. When Nagel's original advisor, Prof. Rohrer, left Berkeley, Prof. Pederson became his advisor. Pederson insisted that CANCER, a proprietary program, be rewritten enough that restrictions could be removed and the program could be put in the public domain.[5]

SPICE1 was first presented at a conference in 1973.[1] SPICE1 was coded in FORTRAN and used nodal analysis to construct the circuit equations. Nodal analysis has limitations in representing inductors, floating voltage sources and the various forms of controlled sources. SPICE1 had relatively few circuit elements available and used a fixed-timestep transient analysis. The real popularity of SPICE started with SPICE2[2] in 1975. SPICE2, also coded in FORTRAN, was a much-improved program with more circuit elements, variable timestep transient analysis using either trapezoidal or the Gear integration method (also known as BDF), equation formulation via modified nodal analysis[6] (avoiding the limitations of nodal analysis), and an innovative FORTRAN-based memory allocation system developed by another graduate student, Ellis Cohen. The last FORTRAN version of SPICE was 2G.6 in

1983. SPICE3[7] was developed by Thomas Quarles (with A. Richard Newton as advisor) in 1989. It is written in C, uses the same netlist syntax, and added X Window System plotting.

As an early open source program, SPICE was widely distributed and used. Its ubiquity became such that "to SPICE a circuit" remains synonymous with circuit simulation.[8] SPICE source code was from the beginning distributed by UC Berkeley for a nominal charge (to cover the cost of magnetic tape). The license originally included distribution restrictions for countries not considered friendly to the USA, but the source code is currently covered by the BSD license.

SPICE inspired and served as a basis for many other circuit simulation programs, in academia, in industry, and in commercial products. The first commercial version of SPICE was ISPICE[9], an interactive version on a timeshare service, National CSS. The most prominent commercial versions of SPICE include HSPICE (originally commercialized by Shawn and Kim Hailey of Meta Software, but now owned by Synopsys) and PSPICE (now owned by Cadence Design Systems). The academic spinoffs of SPICE include XSPICE, developed at Georgia Tech, which added mixed analog/digital "code models" for behavioral simulation, and Cider (previously CODECS, from UC Berkeley/Oregon State Univ.) which added semiconductor device simulation. The integrated circuit industry adopted SPICE quickly, and until commercial versions became well developed many IC design houses had proprietary versions of SPICE.[10] Today a few IC manufacturers, typically the larger companies, have groups continuing to develop SPICE-based circuit simulation programs. Among these are ADICE at Analog Devices, LTspice at Linear Technology, Mica at Freescale Semiconductor, and TISPICE at Texas Instruments. (Other companies maintain internal circuit simulators which are not directly based upon SPICE, among them PowerSpice at IBM, Titan at Qimonda, Lynx at Intel Corporation, and Pstar at NXP Semiconductor.) In addition, starting in the mid-1980s, some EDA companies started to develop what has become known as Fast-SPICE[11], which use the same text netlists and output formats as SPICE, but by employing an event-driven algorithm and table lookup models (among other techniques) trade-off precision for enhanced speed and capacity.

Program features and structure

SPICE became popular because it contained the analyses and models needed to design integrated circuits of the time, and was robust enough and fast enough to be practical to use.[12] Precursors to SPICE often had a single purpose: The BIAS[13] program, for example, did simulation of bipolar transistor circuit operating points; the SLIC[14] program did only small-signal analyses. SPICE combined operating point solutions, transient analysis, and various small-signal analyses with the circuit elements and device models needed to successfully simulate many circuits.

Analyses

SPICE2 included these analyses:

- AC analysis (linear small-signal frequency domain analysis)
- DC analysis (nonlinear quiescent point calculation)
- DC transfer curve analysis (a sequence of nonlinear operating points calculated while sweeping an input voltage or current, or a circuit parameter)
- Noise analysis (a small signal analysis done using an adjoint matrix technique which sums uncorrelated noise currents at a chosen output point)
- Transfer function analysis (a small-signal input/output gain and impedance calculation)
- Transient analysis (time-domain large-signal solution of nonlinear differential algebraic equations)

Since SPICE is generally used to model nonlinear circuits, the small signal analyses are necessarily preceded by a quiescent point calculation at which the circuit is linearized. SPICE2 also contained code for other small-signal analyses: sensitivity analysis, pole-zero analysis, and small-signal distortion analysis. Analysis at various temperatures was done by automatically updating semiconductor model parameters for temperature, allowing the circuit to be simulated at temperature extremes.

Other circuit simulators have since added many analyses beyond those in SPICE2 to address changing industry requirements. Parametric sweeps were added to analyze circuit performance with changing manufacturing tolerances or operating conditions. Loop gain and stability calculations were added for analog circuits. Harmonic balance or time-domain steady state analyses were added for RF and switched-capacitor circuit design. However, a public-domain circuit simulator containing the modern analyses and features needed to become a successor in popularity to SPICE has not yet emerged.[12]

Device models

SPICE2 included many semiconductor device compact models: three levels of MOSFET model, a combined Ebers–Moll and Gummel-Poon bipolar model, a JFET model, and a model for a junction diode. In addition, it had many other elements: resistors, capacitors, inductors (including coupling), independent voltage and current sources, ideal transmission lines, and voltage and current controlled sources.

SPICE3 added more sophisticated MOSFET models, which were required due to advances in semiconductor technology. In particular, the BSIM family of models were added, which were also developed at UC Berkeley.

Commercial and industrial SPICE simulators have added many other device models as technology advanced and earlier models became inaccurate. To attempt standardization of these models so that a set of model parameters may be used in different simulators, an industry working group was formed, the Compact Model Council[15], to choose, maintain and promote the use of standard models [16]. The standard models today include BSIM3 [17], BSIM4 [18], BSIMSOI [19], PSP [20], HICUM [21], and MEXTRAM [22].

Input and output: Netlists, schematic capture and plotting

SPICE2 took a text netlist as input and produced line-printer listings as output, which fit with the computing environment in 1975. These listings were either columns of numbers corresponding to calculated outputs (typically voltages or currents), or line-printer character "plots". SPICE3 retained the netlist for circuit description, but allowed analyses to be controlled from a command-line interface similar to the C shell. SPICE3 also added basic X-Window plotting, as UNIX and engineering workstations became common.

Vendors and various free software projects have added schematic capture front-ends to SPICE, allowing a schematic diagram of the circuit to be drawn and the netlist to be automatically generated. Also, graphical user interfaces were added for selecting the simulations to be done and manipulating the voltage and current output vectors. In addition, very capable graphing utilities have been added to see waveforms and graphs of parametric dependencies. Several free versions of these extended programs are available, some as introductory limited packages, and some without restrictions.

See also

- Circuit simulators with articles on Wikipedia are listed in Category:Electronic circuit simulators
- Advanced Design System Transient Convolution Simulator
- Input Output Buffer Information Specification (IBIS)
- List of free electronics circuit simulators
- Multisim
- PSPICE
- Ngspice
- Spectre Circuit Simulator
- Transistor models

External links

Histories, original papers

- The original SPICE1 paper [23]
- L. W. Nagel's dissertation (SPICE2) [24]
- Thomas Quarles' dissertation (SPICE3) [25]
- Larry Nagel, "The Life of SPICE" [26]
- A brief history of SPICE [27]

Versions with source code available

- SPICE2 and SPICE3 at UC Berkeley [28]
- Cider at UC Berkeley [29]
- ngspice: SPICE3 with updates and XSPICE extensions [30]
- tclspice: ngspice and Tcl scripting [31]
- XSPICE at Georgia Tech [32]
- (Free to use online code)Spice3f4 [33]

Tutorials, user information

- Comprehensive, detailed PSPICE tutorial and user guide at Wilfrid Laurier University, Canada [34]
- The Spice Page [35]
- SPICE on gEDA HOWTO [36]
- Spice 3 Userguide [37]
- Spice 3 Quickstart Tutorial [38]
- Designer's Guide Community [39]
- SPICE Simulation tutorial [40]

Applications

- Sample Spice code and output for various circuits [41]
- NanoDotTek Report NDT14-08-2007, 12 August 2007 [42]

References

[1] Nagel, L. W, and Pederson, D. O., *SPICE (Simulation Program with Integrated Circuit Emphasis)*, Memorandum No. ERL-M382, University of California, Berkeley, Apr. 1973

[2] Nagel, Laurence W., *SPICE2: A Computer Program to Simulate Semiconductor Circuits*, Memorandum No. ERL-M520, University of California, Berkeley, May 1975

[3] Warwick, Colin (May 2009). "Everything you always wanted to know about SPICE* (*But were afraid to ask)" (http://www.nutwooduk.co.uk/pdf/Issue82.PDF#page=27) (PDF). *EMC Journal* (Nutwood UK Limited) (82): 27–29. ISSN 1748-9253. .

[4] Nagel, L. W., and Rohrer, R. A. (August 1971). "Computer Analysis of Nonlinear Circuits, Excluding Radiation" (http://ieeexplore.ieee.org/xpls/abs_all.jsp?arnumber=1050166). *IEEE Journal of Solid State Circuits* **SC-6**: 166–182. doi:10.1109/JSSC.1971.1050166. .

[5] Perry, T. (June 1998). "Donald O. Pederson" (http://ieeexplore.ieee.org/search/wrapper.jsp?arnumber=681968). *IEEE Spectrum* **35**: 22–27. doi:10.1109/6.681968. .

[6] Ho, Ruehli, and Brennan (April 1974). "The Modified Nodal Approach to Network Analysis" (http://ieeexplore.ieee.org/xpls/abs_all.jsp?arnumber=1084079). . pp. 505–509. .

[7] Quarles, Thomas L., *Analysis of Performance and Convergence Issues for Circuit Simulation*, Memorandum No. UCB/ERL M89/42, University of California, Berkeley, Apr. 1989.

[8] Pescovitz, David (2002-05-02). "1972: The release of SPICE, still the industry standard tool for integrated circuit design" (http://www.coe.berkeley.edu/labnotes/0502/history.html). Lab Notes: Research from the Berkeley College of Engineering. . Retrieved 2007-03-10.

[9] Vladimirescu, Andrei, *SPICE -- The Third Decade*, Proc. 1990 IEEE Bipolar Circuits and Technology Meeting, Minneapolis, Sept. 1990, pp. 96–101

[10] K. S. Kundert, *The Designer's Guide to SPICE and SPECTRE*, Kluwer. Academic Publishers, Boston , 1998

[11] AllAboutEDA: Fast-SPICE description (http://www.allabouteda.com/second-generation-circuit-simulation-fast-spice/)

[12] Nagel, L., Is it Time for SPICE4? (http://www.cs.sandia.gov/nacdm/talks/Nagal_Larry_NACDM2004.pdf), 2004 Numerical Aspects of Device and Circuit Modeling Workshop, June 23-25, 2004, Santa Fe, New Mexico. Retrieved on 2007-11-10

[13] McCalla and Howard (February 1971). "BIAS-3 – A program for nonlinear D.C. analysis of bipolar transistor circuits" (http://ieeexplore.ieee.org/xpls/abs_all.jsp?arnumber=1050153). *IEEE J. of Solid State Circuits* **6** (1): 14–19. doi:10.1109/JSSC.1971.1050153. .

[14] Idleman, Jenkins, McCalla and Pederson (August 1971). "SLIC—a simulator for linear integrated circuits" (http://ieeexplore.ieee.org/xpls/abs_all.jsp?arnumber=1050168). *IEEE J. of Solid State Circuits* **6** (4): 188–203. doi:10.1109/JSSC.1971.1050168. .

[15] "CMC - Compact Model Council" (http://www.geia.org/index.asp?bid=597). GEIA. .

C++ (programming language)

The C++ Programming Language, written by its architect, is the seminal book on the language.

Paradigm	Multi-paradigm:[1] procedural, object-oriented, generic
Appeared in	1983
Designed by	Bjarne Stroustrup
Developer	Bjarne Stroustrup Bell Labs ISO/IEC JTC1/SC22/WG21
Stable release	ISO/IEC 14882:2003 (2003)
Preview release	C++0x
Typing discipline	Static, unsafe, nominative
Major implementations	Borland C++ Builder, GCC, Intel C++ Compiler, Microsoft Visual C++, Sun Studio, Turbo C++, Comeau C/C++, clang
Dialects	ISO/IEC C++ 1998, ISO/IEC C++ 2003
Influenced by	C, Simula, Ada 83, ALGOL 68, CLU, ML[1]
Influenced	Perl, LPC, Lua, Pike, Ada 95, Java, PHP, D, C99, C#, Aikido, Falcon
OS	Cross-platform (multi-platform)
Usual file extensions	.h .hh .hpp .hxx .h++ .cc .cpp .cxx .c++
	C++ Programming at Wikibooks

C++ (pronounced *see plus plus*) is a statically typed, free-form, multi-paradigm, compiled, general-purpose programming language. It is regarded as a "middle-level" language, as it comprises a combination of both high-level and low-level language features.[2] It was developed by Bjarne Stroustrup starting in 1979 at Bell Labs as an enhancement to the C programming language and originally named *C with Classes*. It was renamed *C++* in 1983.[3]

As one of the most popular programming languages ever created,[4] [5] C++ is widely used in the software industry. Some of its application domains include systems software, application software, device drivers, embedded software, high-performance server and client applications, and entertainment software such as video games. Several groups provide both free and proprietary C++ compiler software, including the GNU Project, Microsoft, Intel and Borland. C++ has greatly influenced many other popular programming languages, most notably Java.

C++ is also used for hardware design, where design is initially described in C++, then analyzed, architecturally constrained, and scheduled to create a register transfer level hardware description language via high-level synthesis.

The language began as enhancements to C, first adding classes, then virtual functions, operator overloading, multiple inheritance, templates, and exception handling among other features. After years of development, the C++ programming language standard was ratified in 1998 as *ISO/IEC 14882:1998*. That standard is still current, but is amended by the 2003 technical corrigendum, *ISO/IEC 14882:2003*. The next standard version (known informally as

C++0x) is in development.

History

Bjarne Stroustrup began work on "C with Classes" in 1979. The idea of creating a new language originated from Stroustrup's experience in programming for his Ph.D. thesis. Stroustrup found that Simula had features that were very helpful for large software development, but the language was too slow for practical use, while BCPL was fast but too low-level to be suitable for large software development. When Stroustrup started working in AT&T Bell Labs, he had the problem of analyzing the UNIX kernel with respect to distributed computing. Remembering his Ph.D. experience, Stroustrup set out to enhance the C language with Simula-like features. C was chosen because it was general-purpose, fast, portable and widely used. Besides C and Simula,

Bjarne Stroustrup, creator of C++

some other languages that inspired him were ALGOL 68, Ada, CLU and ML. At first, the class, derived class, strong type checking, inlining, and default argument features were added to C via Stroustrup's C++ to C compiler, Cfront. The first commercial implementation of C++ was released in October 1985.[6]

In 1983, the name of the language was changed from *C with Classes* to C++ (++ being the increment operator in C). New features were added including virtual functions, function name and operator overloading, references, constants, user-controlled free-store memory control, improved type checking, and BCPL style single-line comments with two forward slashes (//). In 1985, the first edition of *The C++ Programming Language* was released, providing an important reference to the language, since there was not yet an official standard. Release 2.0 of C++ came in 1989. New features included multiple inheritance, abstract classes, static member functions, const member functions, and protected members. In 1990, *The Annotated C++ Reference Manual* was published. This work became the basis for the future standard. Late addition of features included templates, exceptions, namespaces, new casts, and a Boolean type.

As the C++ language evolved, the standard library evolved with it. The first addition to the C++ standard library was the stream I/O library which provided facilities to replace the traditional C functions such as printf and scanf. Later, among the most significant additions to the standard library, was the Standard Template Library.

C++ continues to be used and is one of the preferred programming languages to develop professional applications. The popularity of the language continues to grow.[7]

Language standard

In 1998, the C++ standards committee (the ISO/IEC JTC1/SC22/WG21 working group) standardized C++ and published the international standard *ISO/IEC 14882:1998* (informally known as *C++98*[8]). For some years after the official release of the standard, the committee processed defect reports, and published a corrected version of the C++ standard, *ISO/IEC 14882:2003*, in 2003. In 2005, a technical report, called the "Library Technical Report 1" (often known as TR1 for short), was released. While not an official part of the standard, it specified a number of extensions to the standard library, which were expected to be included in the next version of C++. Support for TR1 is growing in almost all currently maintained C++ compilers.

The standard for the next version of the language (known informally as C++0x) is in development.

Etymology

According to Stroustrup: "the name signifies the evolutionary nature of the changes from C".[9] During C++'s development period, the language had been referred to as "new C", then "C with Classes". The final name is credited to Rick Mascitti (mid-1983) and was first used in December 1983. When Mascitti was questioned informally in 1992 about the naming, he indicated that it was given in a tongue-in-cheek spirit. It stems from C's "++" operator (which increments the value of a variable) and a common naming convention of using "+" to indicate an enhanced computer program. There is no language called "C plus". ABCL/c+ was the name of an earlier, unrelated programming language.

Philosophy

In *The Design and Evolution of C++* (1994), Bjarne Stroustrup describes some rules that he used for the design of C++:

- C++ is designed to be a statically typed, general-purpose language that is as efficient and portable as C
- C++ is designed to directly and comprehensively support multiple programming styles (procedural programming, data abstraction, object-oriented programming, and generic programming)
- C++ is designed to give the programmer choice, even if this makes it possible for the programmer to choose incorrectly
- C++ is designed to be as compatible with C as possible, therefore providing a smooth transition from C
- C++ avoids features that are platform specific or not general purpose
- C++ does not incur overhead for features that are not used (the "zero-overhead principle")
- C++ is designed to function without a sophisticated programming environment

Stroustrup also mentions that C++ was always intended to make programming more *fun* and that many of the double meanings in the language are intentional.

Inside the C++ Object Model (Lippman, 1996) describes how compilers may convert C++ program statements into an in-memory layout. Compiler authors are, however, free to implement the standard in their own manner.

Standard library

The 1998 ANSI/ISO C++ standard consists of two parts: the core language and the C++ Standard Library; the latter includes most of the Standard Template Library (STL) and a slightly modified version of the C standard library. Many C++ libraries exist which are not part of the standard, and, using linkage specification, libraries can even be written in languages such as C, Fortran, Pascal, or BASIC. Which of these are supported is compiler dependent.

The C++ standard library incorporates the C standard library with some small modifications to make it optimized with the C++ language. Another large part of the C++ library is based on the STL. This provides such useful tools as containers (for example vectors and lists), iterators to provide these containers with array-like access and algorithms to perform operations such as searching and sorting. Furthermore (multi)maps (associative arrays) and (multi)sets are provided, all of which export compatible interfaces. Therefore it is possible, using templates, to write generic algorithms that work with any container or on any sequence defined by iterators. As in C, the features of the library are accessed by using the #include directive to include a standard header. C++ provides 69 standard headers, of which 19 are deprecated.

The STL was originally a third-party library from HP and later SGI, before its incorporation into the C++ standard. The standard does not refer to it as "STL", as it is merely a part of the standard library, but many people still use that term to distinguish it from the rest of the library (input/output streams, internationalization, diagnostics, the C library subset, etc.).

Most C++ compilers provide an implementation of the C++ standard library, including the STL. Compiler-independent implementations of the STL, such as STLPort,[10] also exist. Other projects also produce various custom implementations of the C++ standard library and the STL with various design goals.

Language features

C++ inherits most of C's syntax. The following is Bjarne Stroustrup's version of the Hello world program which uses the C++ standard library stream facility to write a message to standard output:[11] [12]

```
#include <iostream>

int main()
{
    std::cout << "Hello, world!\n";
}
```

Within functions that define a non-void return type, failure to return a value before control reaches the end of the function results in undefined behaviour (compilers typically provide the means to issue a diagnostic in such a case).[13] The sole exception to this rule is the main function, which implicitly returns a value of zero.[14]

Operators and operator overloading

C++ provides more than 30 operators, covering basic arithmetic, bit manipulation, indirection, comparisons, logical operations and others. Almost all operators can be overloaded for user-defined types, with a few notable exceptions such as member access (. and .*). The rich set of overloadable operators is central to using C++ as a domain specific language. The overloadable operators are also an essential part of many advanced C++ programming techniques, such as smart pointers. Overloading an operator does not change the precedence of calculations involving the operator, nor does it change the number of operands that the operator uses (any operand may however be ignored by the operator, though it will be evaluated prior to execution). Overloaded "&&" and "||" operators lose their short-circuit evaluation property.

Templates

C++ templates enable generic programming. C++ supports both function and class templates. Templates may be parameterized by types, compile-time constants, and other templates. C++ templates are implemented by *instantiation* at compile-time. To instantiate a template, compilers substitute specific arguments for a template's parameters to generate a concrete function or class instance. Some substitutions are not possible; these are eliminated by an overload resolution policy described by the phrase "Substitution failure is not an error" (SFINAE). Templates are a powerful tool that can be used for generic programming, template metaprogramming, and code optimization, but this power implies a cost. Template use may increase code size, since each template instantiation produces a copy of the template code: one for each set of template arguments. This is in contrast to run-time generics seen in other languages (e.g. Java) where at compile-time the type is erased and a single template body is preserved.

Templates are different from macros: while both of these compile-time language features enable conditional compilation, templates are not restricted to lexical substitution. Templates are aware of the semantics and type system of their companion language, as well as all compile-time type definitions, and can perform high-level operations including programmatic flow control based on evaluation of strictly type-checked parameters. Macros are capable of conditional control over compilation based on predetermined criteria, but cannot instantiate new types, recurse, or perform type evaluation and in effect are limited to pre-compilation text-substitution and text-inclusion/exclusion. In other words, macros can control compilation flow based on pre-defined symbols but cannot, unlike templates, independently instantiate new symbols. Templates are a tool for static polymorphism (see below) and generic programming.

In addition, templates are a compile time mechanism in C++ which is Turing-complete, meaning that any computation expressible by a computer program can be computed, in some form, by a template metaprogram prior to runtime.

In summary, a template is a compile-time parameterized function or class written without knowledge of the specific arguments used to instantiate it. After instantiation the resulting code is equivalent to code written specifically for the passed arguments. In this manner, templates provide a way to decouple generic, broadly applicable aspects of functions and classes (encoded in templates) from specific aspects (encoded in template parameters) without sacrificing performance due to abstraction.

Objects

C++ introduces object-oriented (OO) features to C. It offers classes, which provide the four features commonly present in OO (and some non-OO) languages: abstraction, encapsulation, inheritance, and polymorphism. Objects are instances of classes created at runtime. The class can be thought of as a template from which many different individual objects may be generated as a program runs.

Encapsulation

Encapsulation is the hiding of information in order to ensure that data structures and operators are used as intended and to make the usage model more obvious to the developer. C++ provides the ability to define classes and functions as its primary encapsulation mechanisms. Within a class, members can be declared as either public, protected, or private in order to explicitly enforce encapsulation. A public member of the class is accessible to any function. A private member is accessible only to functions that are members of that class and to functions and classes explicitly granted access permission by the class ("friends"). A protected member is accessible to members of classes that inherit from the class in addition to the class itself and any friends.

The OO principle is that all of the functions (and only the functions) that access the internal representation of a type should be encapsulated within the type definition. C++ supports this (via member functions and friend functions), but does not enforce it: the programmer can declare parts or all of the representation of a type to be public, and is allowed to make public entities that are not part of the representation of the type. Because of this, C++ supports not just OO programming, but other weaker decomposition paradigms, like modular programming.

It is generally considered good practice to make all data private or protected, and to make public only those functions that are part of a minimal interface for users of the class. This hides all the details of data implementation, allowing the designer to later fundamentally change the implementation without changing the interface in any way.[15] [16]

Inheritance

Inheritance allows one data type to acquire properties of other data types. Inheritance from a base class may be declared as public, protected, or private. This access specifier determines whether unrelated and derived classes can access the inherited public and protected members of the base class. Only public inheritance corresponds to what is usually meant by "inheritance". The other two forms are much less frequently used. If the access specifier is omitted, a "class" inherits privately, while a "struct" inherits publicly. Base classes may be declared as virtual; this is called virtual inheritance. Virtual inheritance ensures that only one instance of a base class exists in the inheritance graph, avoiding some of the ambiguity problems of multiple inheritance.

Multiple inheritance is a C++ feature not found in most other languages. Multiple inheritance allows a class to be derived from more than one base class; this allows for more elaborate inheritance relationships. For example, a "Flying Cat" class can inherit from both "Cat" and "Flying Mammal". Some other languages, such as Java or C#, accomplish something similar (although more limited) by allowing inheritance of multiple interfaces while restricting the number of base classes to one (interfaces, unlike classes, provide only declarations of member functions, no implementation or member data). An interface as in Java and C# can be defined in C++ as a class containing only pure virtual functions, often known as an abstract base class or "ABC". The member functions of such an abstract base classes are normally explicitly defined in the derived class, not inherited implicitly.

Polymorphism

Polymorphism enables one common interface for many implementations, and for objects to act differently under different circumstances.

C++ supports several kinds of *static* (compile-time) and *dynamic* (run-time) polymorphisms. Compile-time polymorphism does not allow for certain run-time decisions, while run-time polymorphism typically incurs a performance penalty.

Static polymorphism

Function overloading allows programs to declare multiple functions having the same name (but with different arguments). The functions are distinguished by the number and/or types of their formal parameters. Thus, the same function name can refer to different functions depending on the context in which it is used. The type returned by the function is not used to distinguish overloaded functions.

When declaring a function, a programmer can specify default value for one or more parameters. Doing so allows the parameters with defaults to optionally be omitted when the function is called, in which case the default arguments will be used. When a function is called with fewer arguments than there are declared parameters, explicit arguments are matched to parameters in left-to-right order, with any unmatched parameters at the end of the parameter list being assigned their default arguments. In many cases, specifying default arguments in a single function declaration is preferable to providing overloaded function definitions with different numbers of parameters.

Templates in C++ provide a sophisticated mechanism for writing generic, polymorphic code. In particular, through the Curiously Recurring Template Pattern it's possible to implement a form of static polymorphism that closely mimics the syntax for overriding virtual functions. Since C++ templates are type-aware and Turing-complete they can also be used to let the compiler resolve recursive conditionals and generate substantial programs through template metaprogramming.

Dynamic polymorphism

Inheritance

Variable pointers (and references) to a base class type in C++ can refer to objects of any derived classes of that type in addition to objects exactly matching the variable type. This allows arrays and other kinds of containers to hold pointers to objects of differing types. Because assignment of values to variables usually occurs at run-time, this is necessarily a run-time phenomenon.

C++ also provides a dynamic_cast operator, which allows the program to safely attempt conversion of an object into an object of a more specific object type (as opposed to conversion to a more general type, which is always allowed). This feature relies on run-time type information (RTTI). Objects known to be of a certain specific type can also be cast to that type with static_cast, a purely compile-time construct which is faster and does not require RTTI.

Virtual member functions

Ordinarily when a function in a derived class overrides a function in a base class, the function to call is determined by the type of the object. A given function is overridden when there exists no difference, in the number or type of parameters, between two or more definitions of that function. Hence, at compile time it may not be possible to determine the type of the object and therefore the correct function to call, given only a base class pointer; the decision is therefore put off until runtime. This is called dynamic dispatch. Virtual member functions or *methods*[17] allow the most specific implementation of the function to be called, according to the actual run-time type of the object. In C++ implementations, this is commonly done using virtual function tables. If the object type is known, this may be bypassed by prepending a fully qualified class name before the function call, but in general calls to virtual functions are resolved at run time.

In addition to standard member functions, operator overloads and destructors can be virtual. A general rule of thumb is that if any functions in the class are virtual, the destructor should be as well. As the type of an object at its creation is known at compile time, constructors, and by extension copy constructors, cannot be virtual. Nonetheless a situation may arise where a copy of an object needs to be created when a pointer to a derived object is passed as a pointer to a base object. In such a case a common solution is to create a clone() (or similar) function and declare that as virtual. The clone() method creates and returns a copy of the derived class when called.

A member function can also be made "pure virtual" by appending it with = 0 after the closing parenthesis and before the semicolon. Objects cannot be created of a class with a pure virtual function and are called abstract data types. Such abstract data types can only be derived from. Any derived class inherits the virtual function as pure and must provide a non-pure definition of it (and all other pure virtual functions) before objects of the derived class can be created. A program that attempts to create an object of a class with a pure virtual member function or inherited pure virtual member function is ill-formed.

Parsing and processing C++ source code

It is relatively difficult to write a good C++ parser with classic parsing algorithms such as LALR(1).[18] This is partly because the C++ grammar is not LALR. Because of this, there are very few tools for analyzing or performing non-trivial transformations (e.g., refactoring) of existing code. One way to handle this difficulty is to choose a different syntax, such as Significantly Prettier and Easier C++ Syntax, which is LALR(1) parsable. More powerful parsers, such as GLR parsers, can be substantially simpler (though slower).

Parsing (in the literal sense of producing a syntax tree) is not the most difficult problem in building a C++ processing tool. Such tools must also have the same understanding of the meaning of the identifiers in the program as a compiler might have. Practical systems for processing C++ must then not only parse the source text, but be able to resolve for each identifier precisely which definition applies (e.g. they must correctly handle C++'s complex scoping rules) and what its type is, as well as the types of larger expressions.

Finally, a practical C++ processing tool must be able to handle the variety of C++ dialects used in practice (such as that supported by the GNU Compiler Collection and that of Microsoft's Visual C++) and implement appropriate analyzers, source code transformers, and regenerate source text. Combining advanced parsing algorithms such as GLR with symbol table construction and program transformation machinery can enable the construction of arbitrary C++ tools.

Compatibility

Producing a reasonably standards-compliant C++ compiler has proven to be a difficult task for compiler vendors in general. For many years, different C++ compilers implemented the C++ language to different levels of compliance to the standard, and their implementations varied widely in some areas such as partial template specialization. Recent releases of most popular C++ compilers support almost all of the C++ 1998 standard.[19]

In order to give compiler vendors greater freedom, the C++ standards committee decided not to dictate the implementation of name mangling, exception handling, and other implementation-specific features. The downside of this decision is that object code produced by different compilers is expected to be incompatible. There are, however, third party standards for particular machines or operating systems which attempt to standardize compilers on those platforms (for example C++ ABI[20]); some compilers adopt a secondary standard for these items.

With C

C++ is often considered to be a superset of C, but this is not strictly true.[21] Most C code can easily be made to compile correctly in C++, but there are a few differences that cause some valid C code to be invalid in C++, or to behave differently in C++.

One commonly encountered difference is that C allows implicit conversion from void* to other pointer types, but C++ does not. Another common portability issue is that C++ defines many new keywords, such as new and class, that may be used as identifiers (e.g. variable names) in a C program.

Some incompatibilities have been removed by the latest (C99) C standard, which now supports C++ features such as // comments and mixed declarations and code. On the other hand, C99 introduced a number of new features that C++ does not support, such as variable-length arrays, native complex-number types, designated initializers and compound literals.[22] However, at least some of the new C99 features will likely be included in the next version of the C++ standard, C++0x.

In order to intermix C and C++ code, any function declaration or definition that is to be called from/used both in C and C++ must be declared with C linkage by placing it within an extern "C" {/*...*/} block. Such a function may not rely on features depending on name mangling (i.e., function overloading).

Criticism

Critics of the language raise several points. First, since C++ includes C as a subset, it inherits many of the criticisms leveled at C. For its large feature set, it is criticized as being over-complicated, and difficult to fully master.[23] Bjarne Stroustrup points out that resultant executables do not support these claims of bloat: "*I have even seen the C++ version of the 'hello world' program smaller than the C version.*"[24] An Embedded C++ standard was proposed to deal with part of this, but criticized for leaving out useful parts of the language that incur no runtime penalty.[25]

Other criticism stems from what is missing from C++. For example, the current version of Standard C++ provides no language features to create multi-threaded software. These facilities are present in some other languages including Java, Ada, and C# (see also Lock). It is possible to use operating system calls or third party libraries to do multi-threaded programming, but both approaches may create portability concerns. The new C++0x standard addresses this matter by extending the language with threading facilities.

C++ is also sometimes compared unfavorably with languages such as Smalltalk, Java, or Eiffel on the basis that it enables programmers to "mix and match" object-oriented programming, procedural programming, generic programming, functional programming, declarative programming, and others, rather than strictly enforcing a single style, although C++ is intentionally a multi-paradigm language.[1]

A fraudulent article was written wherein Bjarne Stroustrup is supposedly interviewed for a 1998 issue of IEEE's 'Computer' magazine[26]. In this article, the interviewer expects to discuss the successes of C++ now that several years had passed after its introduction. Instead, Stroustrup proceeds to confess that his invention of C++ was intended to create the most complex and difficult language possible to weed out amateur programmers and raise the salaries of the few programmers who could master the language. The article contains various criticisms of C++'s complexity and poor usability, most false or exaggerated. In reality, Stroustrup wrote no such article, and due to the pervasiveness of the hoax, was compelled to publish an official denial on his website.[27].

C++ is commonly criticized for lacking built in garbage collection. On his website, Stroustrup explains that automated memory management is routinely implemented directly in C++, without need for a built-in collector, using "smart pointer" classes.[28] Garbage collection not based on reference counting is possible in C++ through external libraries.[29]

See also

- *The C++ Programming Language*
- C++0x, the planned new standard for C++
- Comparison of integrated development environments for C/C++
- Comparison of programming languages
- List of C++ compilers
- List of C++ template libraries
- Comparison of Java and C++

Further reading

- Abrahams, David; Aleksey Gurtovoy. *C++ Template Metaprogramming: Concepts, Tools, and Techniques from Boost and Beyond*. Addison-Wesley. ISBN 0-321-22725-5.
- Alexandrescu, Andrei (2001). *Modern C++ Design: Generic Programming and Design Patterns Applied*. Addison-Wesley. ISBN 0-201-70431-5.
- Alexandrescu, Andrei; Herb Sutter (2004). *C++ Design and Coding Standards: Rules and Guidelines for Writing Programs*. Addison-Wesley. ISBN 0-321-11358-6.
- Becker, Pete (2006). *The C++ Standard Library Extensions : A Tutorial and Reference*. Addison-Wesley. ISBN 0-321-41299-0.
- Brokken, Frank (2010). *C++ Annotations* [30]. University of Groningen. ISBN 90 367 0470 7.
- Coplien, James O. (1992, reprinted with corrections 1994). *Advanced C++: Programming Styles and Idioms*. ISBN 0-201-54855-0.
- Dewhurst, Stephen C. (2005). *C++ Common Knowledge: Essential Intermediate Programming*. Addison-Wesley. ISBN 0-321-32192-8.
- Information Technology Industry Council (15 October 2003). *Programming languages — C++* (Second edition ed.). Geneva: ISO/IEC. 14882:2003(E).
- Josuttis, Nicolai M. *The C++ Standard Library*. Addison-Wesley. ISBN 0-201-37926-0.
- Koenig, Andrew; Barbara E. Moo (2000). *Accelerated C++ - Practical Programming by Example*. Addison-Wesley. ISBN 0-201-70353-X.
- Lippman, Stanley B.; Josée Lajoie, Barbara E. Moo (2005). *C++ Primer*. Addison-Wesley. ISBN 0-201-72148-1.
- Lippman, Stanley B. (1996). *Inside the C++ Object Model*. Addison-Wesley. ISBN 0-201-83454-5.
- Stroustrup, Bjarne (2000). *The C++ Programming Language* (Special Edition ed.). Addison-Wesley. ISBN 0-201-70073-5.
- Stroustrup, Bjarne (1994). *The Design and Evolution of C++*. Addison-Wesley. ISBN 0-201-54330-3.
- Stroustrup, Bjarne. *Programming Principles and Practice Using C++*. Addison-Wesley. ISBN 0321543726.
- Sutter, Herb (2001). *More Exceptional C++: 40 New Engineering Puzzles, Programming Problems, and Solutions*. Addison-Wesley. ISBN 0-201-70434-X.
- Sutter, Herb (2004). *Exceptional C++ Style*. Addison-Wesley. ISBN 0-201-76042-8.
- Vandevoorde, David; Nicolai M. Josuttis (2003). *C++ Templates: The complete Guide*. Addison-Wesley. ISBN 0-201-73484-2.
- Scott Meyers (2005). *Effective C++*. Third Edition. Addison-Wesley. ISBN 0-321-33487-6

External links

- JTC1/SC22/WG21 [31] - The ISO/IEC C++ Standard Working Group
  - n3092.pdf [32] - Final Committee Draft of "ISO/IEC IS 14882 - Programming Languages - C++" (26 March 2010)
- A paper by Stroustrup showing the timeline of C++ evolution (1979-1991) [33]
- Bjarne Stroustrup's C++ Style and Technique FAQ [34]
- C++ FAQ Lite by Marshall Cline [35]
- Computer World interview with Bjarne Stroustrup [36]
- CrazyEngineers.com interview with Bjarne Stroustrup [37]
- The State of the Language: An Interview with Bjarne Stroustrup (August 15, 2008) [38]
- Code practices for not breaking binary compatibility between releases of C++ libraries [39] (from KDE Techbase)

References

[1] Stroustrup, Bjarne (1997). "1". *The C++ Programming Language* (Third ed.). ISBN 0201889544. OCLC 59193992.

[2] C++ The Complete Reference Third Edition, Herbert Schildt, Publisher: Osborne McGraw-Hill.

[3] ATT.com (http://www2.research.att.com/~bs/bs_faq.html#invention)

[4] "Programming Language Popularity" (http://www.langpop.com/). 2009. . Retrieved 2009-01-16.

[5] "TIOBE Programming Community Index" (http://www.tiobe.com/index.php/content/paperinfo/tpci/index.html). 2009. . Retrieved 2009-05-06.

[6] "Bjarne Stroustrup's FAQ — When was C++ invented?" (http://public.research.att.com/~bs/bs_faq.html#invention). . Retrieved 30 May 2006.

[7] "Trends on C++ Programmers, Developers & Engineers" (http://www.odesk.com/trends/c++). . Retrieved 1 December 2008.

[8] Stroustrup, Bjarne. "C++ Glossary" (http://www.research.att.com/~bs/glossary.html). . Retrieved 8 June 2007.

[9] "Bjarne Stroustrup's FAQ — Where did the name "C++" come from?" (http://public.research.att.com/~bs/bs_faq.html#name). . Retrieved 16 January 2008.

[10] STLPort home page (http://www.stlport.org/), quote from "The C++ Standard Library" by Nicolai M. Josuttis, p138., ISBN 0-201 37926-0, Addison-Wesley, 1999: "An exemplary version of STL is the STLport, which is available for free for any platform"

[11] Stroustrup, Bjarne (2000). *The C++ Programming Language* (Special Edition ed.). Addison-Wesley. p. 46. ISBN 0-201-70073-5.

[12] Open issues for The C++ Programming Language (3rd Edition) (http://www.research.att.com/~bs/3rd_issues.html) - This code is copied directly from Bjarne Stroustrup's errata page (p. 633). He addresses the use of '\n' rather than std::endl. Also see www.research.att.com (http://www.research.att.com/~bs/bs_faq2.html#void-main) for an explanation of the implicit return 0; in the main function, This implicit return is *not* available in other functions.

[13] ISO/IEC (2003). *ISO/IEC 14882:2003(E): Programming Languages - C++ §6.6.3 The return statement [stmt.return]* para. 2

[14] ISO/IEC (2003). *ISO/IEC 14882:2003(E): Programming Languages - C++ §3.6.1 Main function [basic.start.main]* para. 5

[15] Sutter, Herb; Alexandrescu, Andrei (2004). *C++ Coding Standards: 101 Rules, Guidelines, and Best Practices.* Addison-Wesley.

[16] Henricson, Mats; Nyquist, Erik (1997). *Industrial Strength C++.* Prentice Hall. ISBN ISBN 0-13-120965-5.

[17] Stroustrup, Bjarne (2000). *The C++ Programming Language* (Special Edition ed.). Addison-Wesley. p. 310. ISBN 0-201-70073-5. "A virtual member function is sometimes called a *method*."

[18] Andrew Birkett. "Parsing C++ at nobugs.org" (http://www.nobugs.org/developer/parsingcpp/). Nobugs.org. . Retrieved 3 July 2009.

[19] Herb Sutter (15 April 2003). "C++ Conformance Roundup" (http://www.ddj.com/dept/cpp/184401381). *Dr. Dobb's Journal.* . Retrieved 30 May 2006.

[20] "C++ ABI" (http://www.codesourcery.com/cxx-abi/). . Retrieved 30 May 2006.

[21] "Bjarne Stroustrup's FAQ - Is C a subset of C++?" (http://public.research.att.com/~bs/bs_faq.html#C-is-subset). . Retrieved 18 January 2008.

[22] "C9X -- The New C Standard" (http://home.datacomm.ch/t_wolf/tw/c/c9x_changes.html). . Retrieved 27 December 2008.

[23] Morris, Richard (July 2, 2009). "Niklaus Wirth: Geek of the Week" (http://www.simple-talk.com/opinion/geek-of-the-week/niklaus-wirth-geek-of-the-week/). . Retrieved 8 August 2009. "C++ is a language that was designed to cater to everybody's perceived needs. As a result, the language and even more so its implementations have become complex and bulky, difficult to understand, and likely to contain errors for ever."

[24] Why is the code generated for the "Hello world" program ten times larger for C++ than for C? (http://www.research.att.com/~bs/bs_faq.html#Hello-world)

[25] What do you think of EC++? (http://www.research.att.com/~bs/bs_faq.html#EC++)

[26] Unattributed. Previously unpublished interview with Bjarne Stroustrup, designer of C++ (http://flinflon.brandonu.ca/dueck/1997/62285/stroustroup.html).

[27] Stroustrup, Bjarne. Stroustrup FAQ: Did you really give an interview to IEEE? (http://www2.research.att.com/~bs/bs_faq.html#IEEE)

[28] http://www2.research.att.com/~bs/bs_faq.html.

[29] http://www.hpl.hp.com/personal/Hans_Boehm/gc/

Electronic design automation

Electronic design automation (also known as EDA or ECAD) is a category of software tools for designing electronic systems such as printed circuit boards and integrated circuits. The tools work together in a design flow that chip designers use to design and analyze entire semiconductor chips.

This article describes EDA specifically with respect to integrated circuits.

PCB layout program

History

Early days

Before EDA, integrated circuits were designed by hand, and manually laid out. Some advanced shops used geometric software to generate the tapes for the Gerber photoplotter, but even those copied digital recordings of mechanically-drawn components. The process was fundamentally graphic, with the translation from electronics to graphics done manually. The best known company from this era was Calma, whose GDSII format survives.

By the mid-70s, developers started to automate the design, and not just the drafting. The first placement and routing (Place and route) tools were developed. The proceedings of the Design Automation Conference cover much of this era.

The next era began about the time of the publication of "Introduction to VLSI Systems" by Carver Mead and Lynn Conway in 1980. This ground breaking text advocated chip design with programming languages that compiled to silicon. The immediate result was a considerable increase in the complexity of the chips that could be designed, with improved access to design verification tools that used logic simulation. Often the chips were easier to lay out and more likely to function correctly, since their designs could be simulated more thoroughly prior to construction. Although the languages and tools have evolved, this general approach of specifying the desired behavior in a textual programming language and letting the tools derive the detailed physical design remains the basis of digital IC design today.

The earliest EDA tools were produced academically. One of the most famous was the "Berkeley VLSI Tools Tarball", a set of UNIX utilities used to design early VLSI systems. Still widely used is the Espresso heuristic logic minimizer and Magic.

Another crucial development was the formation of MOSIS, a consortium of universities and fabricators that developed an inexpensive way to train student chip designers by producing real integrated circuits. The basic concept was to use reliable, low-cost, relatively low-technology IC processes, and pack a large number of projects per wafer, with just a few copies of each projects' chips. Cooperating fabricators either donated the processed wafers, or sold them at cost, seeing the program as helpful to their own long-term growth.

Birth of commercial EDA

1981 marks the beginning of EDA as an industry. For many years, the larger electronic companies, such as Hewlett Packard, Tektronix, and Intel, had pursued EDA internally. In 1981, managers and developers spun out of these companies to concentrate on EDA as a business. Daisy Systems, Mentor Graphics, and Valid Logic Systems were all founded around this time, and collectively referred to as **DMV**. Within a few years there were many companies specializing in EDA, each with a slightly different emphasis.

In 1986, Verilog, a popular high-level design language, was first introduced as a hardware description language by Gateway Design Automation. In 1987, the U.S. Department of Defense funded creation of VHDL as a specification language. Simulators quickly followed these introductions, permitting direct simulation of chip designs: executable specifications. In a few more years, back-ends were developed to perform logic synthesis.

Current status

Current digital flows are extremely modular (see Integrated circuit design, Design closure, and Design flow (EDA)). The front ends produce standardized design descriptions that compile into invocations of "cells,", without regard to the cell technology. Cells implement logic or other electronic functions using a particular integrated circuit technology. Fabricators generally provide libraries of components for their production processes, with simulation models that fit standard simulation tools. Analog EDA tools are far less modular, since many more functions are required, they interact more strongly, and the components are (in general) less ideal.

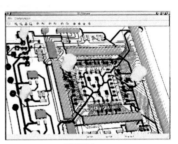

3D PCB layout

EDA for electronics has rapidly increased in importance with the continuous scaling of semiconductor technology. Some users are foundry operators, who operate the semiconductor fabrication facilities, or "fabs", and design-service companies who use EDA software to evaluate an incoming design for manufacturing readiness. EDA tools are also used for programming design functionality into FPGAs.

Software focuses

Design

- High-level synthesis(syn. behavioural synthesis, algorithmic synthesis) For digital chips
- Logic synthesis translation of abstract, logical language such as Verilog or VHDL into a discrete netlist of logic-gates
- Schematic Capture For standard cell digital, analog, rf like Capture CIS in Orcad by CADENCE and ISIS in Proteus
- Layout like Layout in Orcad by Cadence, ARES in Proteus

Simulation

- Transistor simulation – low-level transistor-simulation of a schematic/layout's behavior, accurate at device-level.
- Logic simulation – digital-simulation of an RTL or gate-netlist's digital (boolean 0/1) behavior, accurate at boolean-level.
- **Behavioral Simulation** – high-level simulation of a design's architectural operation, accurate at cycle-level or interface-level.
- Hardware emulation – Use of special purpose hardware to emulate the logic of a proposed design. Can sometimes be plugged into a system in place of a yet-to-be-built chip; this is called **in-circuit emulation**.
- Technology CAD simulate and analyze the underlying process technology. Electrical properties of devices are derived directly from device physics.
- Electromagnetic field solvers, or just field solvers, solve Maxwell's equations directly for cases of interest in IC and PCB design. They are known for being slower but more accurate than the layout extraction above.

Analysis and verification

- Functional verification
- Clock Domain Crossing Verification (CDC check): Similar to linting, but these checks/tools specialize in detecting and reporting potential issues like data loss, meta-stability due to use of multiple clock domains in the design.
- Formal verification, also model checking: Attempts to prove, by mathematical methods, that the system has certain desired properties, and that certain undesired effects (such as deadlock) cannot occur.

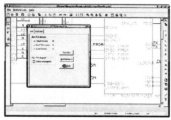

Schematic capture program

- Equivalence checking: algorithmic comparison between a chip's RTL-description and synthesized gate-netlist, to ensure functional equivalence at the *logical* level.
- Static timing analysis: Analysis of the timing of a circuit in an input-independent manner, hence finding a worst case over all possible inputs.
- Physical verification, PV: checking if a design is physically manufacturable, and that the resulting chips will not have any function-preventing physical defects, and will meet original specifications.

Manufacturing preparation

- Mask data preparation, MDP: generation of actual lithography photomask used to physically manufacture the chip.
  - Resolution enhancement techniques, RET – methods of increasing of quality of final photomask.
  - Optical proximity correction, OPC – up-front compensation for diffraction and interference effects occurring later when chip is manufactured using this mask.
  - Mask generation – generation of flat mask image from hierarchical design.
  - Automatic test pattern generation, ATPG – generates pattern-data to systematically exercise as many logic-gates, and other components, as possible.
  - Built-in self-test, or BIST – installs self-contained test-controllers to automatically test a logic (or memory) structure in the design

Companies

Top companies

- $3.41 billion - Synopsys
- $1.82 billion - Cadence
- $806 million - Mentor Graphics
- $188 million - Zuken Inc.
- $135 million - Magma Design Automation

Note: Market caps current as of March, 2010.[1] EEsof should likely be one this list, but does not have a market cap as it is the EDA division of Agilent.

PCB layout and schematic for connector design

Acquisitions

Many of the EDA companies acquire small companies with software or other technology that can be adapted to their core business.[2] Most of the market leaders are rather incestuous amalgamations of many smaller companies. This trend is helped by the tendency of software companies to design tools as accessories that fit naturally into a larger vendor's suite of programs (on digital circuitry, many new tools incorporate analog design, and mixed systems. This is happening because there is now a trend to place entire electronic systems on a single chip.

See also

- Circuit Design
- EDA Software Category

References

[1] http://www.google.com/finance?q=TYO:6947,NASDAQ:LAVA,NASDAQ:MENT,NASDAQ:SNPS,NASDAQ:CDNS
[2] Kirti Sikri Desai (2006). "EDA Innovation through Merger and Acquisitions" (http://www10.edacafe.com/nbc/articles/view_article. php?articleid=301031&interstitial_displayed=Yes). EDA Cafe. . Retrieved March 23, 2010.

Notes

- http://www.staticfreesoft.com/documentsTextbook.html Computer Aids for VLSI Design by Steven M. Rubin
- *Electronic Design Automation For Integrated Circuits Handbook*, by Lavagno, Martin, and Scheffer, ISBN 0-8493-3096-3, 2006
- *Combinatorial Algorithms for Integrated Circuit Layout*, by Thomas Lengauer, ISBN 3-519-02110-2, Teubner Verlag, 1997.
- *The Electronic Design Automation Handbook*, by Dirk Jansen et al., Kluwer Academic Publishers, ISBN 1-4020-7502-2, 2003, available also in German ISBN 3-446-21288-4 (2005)

External links

- EDA Consortium (http://www.edac.org/)
- EDA Industry Working Groups (http://www.eda.org)

Biquad filter

WARNING: Article could not be rendered - ouputting plain text.
Potential causes of the problem are: (a) a bug in the pdf-writer software (b) problematic Mediawiki markup (c) table is too wide

An electronic filter Topology (electronics)topology is an electronic analog filter circuit in which the values of the components remain undefined. A particular topology is then characterized entirely by the manner in which the components are connected, and not by their values.There are many different types of electronic filters and they are characterized by their transfer function, but not by any particular topology. Once the transfer function for a filter is chosen, it remains to select the particular topology to implement that filter. For example, one might choose to design a Butterworth filter using the Sallen–Key topology. Passive topologies A passive topology is one which uses only passive components in its implementation. By passive components it is meant only components that do not, either in reality or in their equivalent circuit due to non-linearity, contain a generator of energy. In electronics terms, this means that all the components are capacitors and inductors and also, in some topologies, resistors. In virtually all cases, passive electronic filters are built up with simple two-port networks called sections. These are invariably connected in a cascade topology and may be multiple repeats of the same section or completely different sections. There is no formal definition of what constitutes a section, but as a minimum it must have one series component and one shunt component. Two sections consisting of just series components could be combined into a single element by impedances in series and an analogous argument applies to shunt components. Typically, filters designed using Network synthesis filtersnetwork synthesis methods will repeat the topology from section to section but the component values will change at each section. The section used is invariably the simplest form of L-section. Composite image filtersImage designed filters on the other hand, keep the same basic component values from section to section but the topology can vary along the filter. Image design tends to make use of the more complex sections. L-sections are never symmetrical, but two L-sections back-to-back form a symmetrical topology and many other sections are symmetrical in form. Ladder topologies Ladder topology is often called Cauer topology after Wilhelm Cauer (inventor of the Elliptical filter), but the topology was, in fact, first used by George Ashley CampbellGeorge Campbell (inventor of the Constant k filter). Campbell published in 1922 but had clearly been using the topology for some time before this. Cauer first picked up on ladders (published 1926) inspired by the work of Foster (1924) Cauer topology is usually thought of as being an unbalanced ladder topology. However, there are two forms of basic ladder topologies;Unbalanced ladder topology Balanced ladder topology A ladder network is a topology built up of cascaded asymmetrical L-sections (unbalanced) or C-sections (balanced). In its lowpass bandform, the ladder topology would consist of series inductors and shunt capacitors. Other bandforms would have an equally simple topology prototype filter#Bandform transformationtransformed from the lowpass topology. Or to put it another way, the shunt admittance is always a dual impedancedual network of the series impedance. Filters built with ladder topology that consist of only one or two filter sections are given special names. These include the L-section, T-section and Π-section (unbalanced filters) and the C-section, H-section and box-section (balanced filters). The chart below shows these various topologies in terms of general constant k filters. They can of course, be used to implement any kind of filter. Image impedanceImage filter sections Unbalanced L Half section T Section Π Section Ladder network Balanced C Half-section H Section Box Section Ladder network X Section (mid-T-Derived) X Section (mid-Π-Derived) N.B. Textbooks and design drawings usually show the unbalanced implementations, but in telecoms it is often required to convert the design to the balanced implementation when used with balanced lines. Modified ladder topologiesseries m-derived topology In image filter design it is common to use topologies that are a modification of the basic ladder topology. These topologies, invented by Otto Zobel,Zobel, 1923 have the same bandform (ie, the same passbands) as the prototype ladder on which they are based but the transfer function is modified to improve some parameter such as impedance matching, stopband rejection or passband to stopband transition steepness. Usually, the design begins with the simple ladder topology and then some transform is applied to it. The resulting topology is ladderlike but no longer obeys the rule that shunt admittances are the dual network of series impedances. The topology invariably becomes more complex and requires higher component counts. These topologies can include; m-derived filtermm'-type filterGeneral mn-type filterGeneral mn-type filterThe m-type (m-derived) filter is by far the most commonly used modified image ladder topology. There are, in fact, two m-type topologies for each of the basic ladder topologies. These are the series derived and shunt derived topologies. These have identical transfer functions to each other but different image impedances. Where a filter is being designed with more than one passband, the m-type topology will result in a filter where each passband has an analogous frequency domain response. It is possible to generalise the m-type topology for filters with more than one passband using parameters m1, m2, m3 etc which are not equal to each other resulting in general mn-typeThere is no universally recognised name for this kind of filter. Zobel (1923) p11 uses the title General Wave-filters having any Pre-assigned Transmitting and Attenuating Bands and Propagation Constants Adjustable Without Changing one Mid-point Characteristic Impedance, which is not very handy to use in an article. Since Zobel refers to the parameters as m1, m2 etc., the shorthand general mn-type seems reasonable terminology to use here. filters which have bandforms which can be dissimilar in different parts of the frequency spectrum. The mm'-type topology can be thought of as a double m-type design. As with the m-type, it has the same bandform but improved transfer characteristics beyond the improvements achieved by m-types. It is, however, a rarely used design due to the drawback of increased component count and complexity. It also has the disadvantage of normally requiring that basic ladder sections and m-type sections are also present in the same filter for impedance matching reasons. In other words, it would normally only ever be found in a Composite image filtercomposite filter. Bridged-T topologiesTypical bridged-T Zobel network equaliser used to correct high end roll-off Zobel constant resistance filtersZobel, 1928 use a topology that is somewhat different from other filter types. These kinds of filters are distinguished by having a constant input resistance at all frequencies and unusually use resistive components in the design of their sections. The higher component and section count of these designs usually limits their use to equalisation applications. The topologies that are usually associated with constant resistance filters are bridged-T and its variants, all described in the Zobel network article: Bridged-T topology Balanced bridged-T topology Open-circuit L-section topology Short-circuit L-section topology Balanced open-circuit C-section topology Balanced short-circuit C-section topology The bridged-T topology is also used to build sections intended to produce a signal delay. In the case of delay sections, there are no resistive components used in the design. Lattice topologyLattice topology X-section phase correction filter Both the T-section from ladder topology and the bridge-T from Zobel topology can be transformed into a lattice topology filter section. However, in both cases this results in a filter with higher component count and complexity so it does not see much general purpose use. The most common application of lattice filters (X-sections) is in all-pass filters used for Lattice phase equaliserphase equalisation.Zobel, 1931Although T and bridged-T sections can always be transformed into X-sections, the reverse is not always possible. This is because of the possibility of negative values of inductance and capacitance arising in the transform. Lattice topology is identical to the more familiar bridge topology, the difference being merely the drawn representation on the page rather than any real difference in topology, cicuitry or function.Active topologiesMultiple feedback topologyMultiple feedback topology circuit.Multiple feedback topology is an electronic filter topology which is used to implement an electronic filter by adding two poles to the transfer function. A diagram of the circuit topology for a second order low pass filter is shown in the figure on the right.The transfer function of the multiple feedback topology circuit, like all second-order linear filters, is: $H(s) = \frac{V_o}{V_i} = -\frac{1}{As^2+Bs+C} = \frac{K \omega^{2}_{0}}{s^{2}+\frac{\omega_{0}}{Q}s+\omega^{2}_{0}}$. In an MF filter, $A = (R_1 R_3 C_2 C_5)$, $B = R_3 C_5 + R_1 C_5 + R_1 R_3 C_5 / R_4$, $C = R_1/R_4$, $Q = \frac{\sqrt{R_3 R_4 C_2 C_5}}{(R_4 + R_3 + |K| R_3)C_5}$ is the Q factor. $K = -R_4/R_1$, is the DC voltage gain, $\omega_{0} = 2 \pi f_{0} = 1 / \sqrt{R_3 R_4 C_2}$

C_5} is the corner frequency Biquad filterFor the digital implementation of a biquad filter, check Digital biquad filterdigital biquad filter.A biquad filter is a type of linear filter that implements a transfer function that is the ratio of two quadratic functions. The name biquad is short for biquadratic. Biquad filters are typically active filteractive and implemented with a single-amplifier biquad (SAB) or two-integrator-loop topology. The SAB topology uses feedback to generate complex numbercomplex Pole (complex analysis)poles and possibly complex Zero (complex analysis)zeros. In particular, the feedback moves the real numberreal poles of an RC circuit in order to generate the proper filter characteristics. The two-integrator-loop topology is derived from rearranging a biquadratic transfer function. The rearrangement will equate one signal with the sum of another signal, its integral, and the integral's integral. In other words, the rearrangement reveals a state variable filter structure. By using different states as outputs, any kind of second-order filter can be implemented. The SAB topology is sensitive to component choice and can be more difficult to adjust. Hence, usually the term biquad refers to the two-integrator-loop state variable filter topology.Tow-Thomas Biquad Example For example, the basic configuration in Figure 1 can be used as either a low-pass filterlow-pass or band-pass filterbandpass filter depending on where the output signal is taken from. Figure 1: The common Tow-Thomas biquad filter topology. The second-order low-pass transfer function is given by $H(s)=\frac{G_{lpf}\omega^{2}_{0}}{s^{2}+\frac{\omega_{0}}{Q}s+\omega^{2}_{0}}$ where low-pass gain $G_{lpf}=R_{2}/R_{1}$. The second-order bandpass transfer function is given by $H(s)=\frac{G_{bpf}\frac{\omega_{0}}{Q}s}{s^{2}+\frac{\omega_{0}}{Q}s+\omega^{2}_{0}}$. with bandpass gain $G_{bpf}=-R_{4}/R_{2}$. In both cases, the Natural frequency is $\omega_{0}=1/\sqrt{R_{2}R_{4}C_{1}C_{2}}$. Quality factor is $Q=\sqrt{\frac{R_{3}^{2}C_{1}}{R_{2}R_{4}C_{2}}}$. The bandwidth is approximated by $B=\omega_{0}/Q$, and Q is sometimes expressed as a damping constant $\zeta=1/2Q$. If a noninverting low-pass filter is required, the output can be taken at the output of the second operational amplifier. If a noninverting bandpass filter is required, the order of the second integrator and the inverter can be switched, and the output taken at the output of the inverter's operational amplifier. See alsoPrototype filterTopology (electronics)Linear filterState variable filterReferencesCampbell, G A, "Physical Theory of the Electric Wave-Filter", Bell Systems Technical Journal, November 1922, vol. 1, no. 2, pp. 1-32.Zobel, O J, "Theory and Design of Uniform and Composite Electric Wave Filters", Bell Systems Technical Journal, Vol. 2 (1923).Foster, R M, "A reactance theorem", Bell Systems Technical Journal, Vol. 3, pp. 259–267, 1924.Cauer, W, "Die Verwirklichung der Wechselstromwiderst ande vorgeschriebener Frequenzabh angigkeit", Archiv f¨ur Elektrotechnik, 17, pp. 355–388, 1926.Zobel, O J, "Distortion correction in electrical networks with constant resistance recurrent networks", Bell Systems Technical Journal, Vol. 7 (1928), p. 438.Zobel, O J, Phase-shifting network, US patent 1 792 523, filed 12 March 1927, issued 17 Feb 1931.

Complex frequency

In mathematics and engineering, the **S plane** is the name for the complex plane on which Laplace transforms are graphed. It is a mathematical domain where, instead of viewing processes in the time domain modelled with time-based functions, they are viewed as equations in the frequency domain. It is used as a graphical analysis tool in engineering and physics.

A real time function is translated into the 's' plane by taking the integral of the function, multiplied by e^{-st} from $-\infty$ to ∞, where s is a complex number.

$$\int_{-\infty}^{\infty} f(t)e^{-st}\, dt$$

One way to understand what this equation is doing is to remember how Fourier analysis works. In Fourier analysis, harmonic sine and cosine waves are multiplied into the signal, and the resultant integration provides indication of a signal present at that frequency (i.e. the signal's energy at a point in the frequency domain). The 's' transform does the same thing, but more generally. The e^{-st} not only catches frequencies, but also the real e^{-t} effects as well. 's' transforms therefore cater not only for frequency response, but decay effects as well. For instance, a damped sine wave can be modelled correctly using 's' transforms.

's' transforms are commonly known as Laplace transforms. In the 's' plane, multiplying by s has the effect of differentiating in the corresponding real time domain. Dividing by s integrates.

Analysing the complex roots of an 's' plane equation and plotting them on an Argand diagram, can reveal information about the frequency response and stability of a real time system.

External links

- Illustration of how the s-plane maps to the z-plane [1]

Circuit analysis

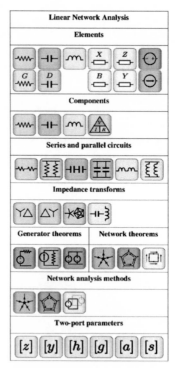

A network, in the context of electronics, is a collection of interconnected components. **Network analysis** is the process of finding the voltages across, and the currents through, every component in the network. There are a number of different techniques for achieving this. However, for the most part, they assume that the components of the network are all linear. The methods described in this article are only applicable to *linear* network analysis except where explicitly stated.

Definitions

Component	A device with two or more terminals into which, or out of which, charge may flow.
Node	A point at which terminals of more than two components are joined. A conductor with a substantially zero resistance is considered to be a node for the purpose of analysis.
Branch	The component(s) joining two nodes.
Mesh	A group of branches within a network joined so as to form a complete loop.
Port	Two terminals where the current into one is identical to the current out of the other.
Circuit	A current from one terminal of a generator, through load component(s) and back into the other terminal. A circuit is, in this sense, a one-port network and is a trivial case to analyse. If there is any connection to any other circuits then a non-trivial network has been formed and at least two ports must exist. Often, "circuit" and "network" are used interchangeably, but many analysts reserve "network" to mean an idealised model consisting of ideal components.[1]
Transfer function	The relationship of the currents and/or voltages between two ports. Most often, an input port and an output port are discussed and the transfer function is described as gain or attenuation.
Component transfer function	For a two-terminal component (i.e. one-port component), the current and voltage are taken as the input and output and the transfer function will have units of impedance or admittance (it is usually a matter of arbitrary convenience whether voltage or current is considered the input). A three (or more) terminal component effectively has two (or more) ports and the transfer function cannot be expressed as a single impedance. The usual approach is to express the transfer function as a matrix of parameters. These parameters can be impedances, but there is a large number of other approaches, see two-port network.

Equivalent circuits

A useful procedure in network analysis is to simplify the network by reducing the number of components. This can be done by replacing the actual components with other notional components that have the same effect. A particular technique might directly reduce the number of components, for instance by combining impedances in series. On the other hand it might merely change the form in to one in which the components can be reduced in a later operation. For instance, one might transform a voltage generator into a current generator using Norton's theorem in order to be able to later combine the internal resistance of the generator with a parallel impedance load.

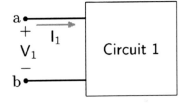

A resistive circuit is a circuit containing only resistors, ideal current sources, and ideal voltage sources. If the sources are constant (DC) sources, the result is a DC circuit. The analysis of a circuit refers to the process of solving for the voltages and currents present in the circuit. The solution principles outlined here also apply to phasor analysis of AC circuits.

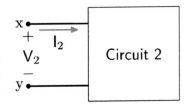

Two circuits are said to be **equivalent** with respect to a pair of terminals if the voltage across the terminals and current through the terminals for one network have the same relationship as the voltage and current at the terminals of the other network.

If $V_2 = V_1$ implies $I_2 = I_1$ for all (real) values of V_1, then with respect to terminals ab and xy, circuit 1 and circuit 2 are equivalent.

The above is a sufficient definition for a one-port network. For more than one port, then it must be defined that the currents and voltages between all pairs of corresponding ports must bear the same relationship. For instance, star and delta networks are effectively three port networks and hence require three simultaneous equations to fully specify their equivalence.

Impedances in series and in parallel

Any two terminal network of impedances can eventually be reduced to a single impedance by successive applications of impedances in series or impendances in parallel.

Impedances in series: $Z_{eq} = Z_1 + Z_2 + \cdots + Z_n$.

Impedances in parallel: $\dfrac{1}{Z_{eq}} = \dfrac{1}{Z_1} + \dfrac{1}{Z_2} + \cdots + \dfrac{1}{Z_n}$.

The above simplified for only two impedances in parallel: $Z_{eq} = \dfrac{Z_1 Z_2}{Z_1 + Z_2}$.

Delta-wye transformation

A network of impedances with more than two terminals cannot be reduced to a single impedance equivalent circuit. An n-terminal network can, at best, be reduced to n impedances. For a three terminal network, the three impedances can be expressed as a three node delta (Δ) network or a four node star (Y) network. These two networks are equivalent and the transformations between them are given below. A general network with an arbitrary number of terminals cannot be reduced to the minimum number of impedances

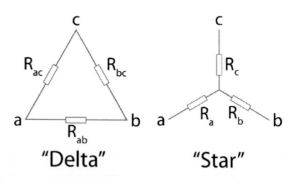

"Delta"   "Star"

using only series and parallel combinations. In general, Y-Δ and Δ-Y transformations must also be used. It can be shown that this is sufficient to find the minimal network for any arbitrary network with successive applications of series, parallel, Y-Δ and Δ-Y; no more complex transformations are required.

For equivalence, the impedances between any pair of terminals must be the same for both networks, resulting in a set of three simultaneous equations. The equations below are expressed as resistances but apply equally to the general case with impedances.

Delta-to-star transformation equations

$$R_a = \frac{R_{ac} R_{ab}}{R_{ac} + R_{ab} + R_{bc}}$$

$$R_b = \frac{R_{ab} R_{bc}}{R_{ac} + R_{ab} + R_{bc}}$$

$$R_c = \frac{R_{bc} R_{ac}}{R_{ac} + R_{ab} + R_{bc}}$$

Star-to-delta transformation equations

$$R_{ac} = \frac{R_a R_b + R_b R_c + R_c R_a}{R_b}$$

$$R_{ab} = \frac{R_a R_b + R_b R_c + R_c R_a}{R_c}$$

$$R_{bc} = \frac{R_a R_b + R_b R_c + R_c R_a}{R_a}$$

General form of network node elimination

The star-to-delta and series-resistor transformations are special cases of the general resistor network node elimination algorithm. Any node connected by N resistors ($R_1 .. R_N$) to nodes $1 .. N$ can be replaced by $\binom{N}{2}$ resistors interconnecting the remaining N nodes. The resistance between any two nodes x and y is given by:

$$R_{xy} = R_x R_y \sum_{i=1}^{N} \frac{1}{R_i}$$

For a star-to-delta ($N = 3$) this reduces to:

$$R_{ab} = R_a R_b \left(\frac{1}{R_a} + \frac{1}{R_b} + \frac{1}{R_c} \right) = \frac{R_a R_b (R_a R_b + R_a R_c + R_b R_c)}{R_a R_b R_c} = \frac{R_a R_b + R_b R_c + R_c R_a}{R_c}$$

For a series reduction ($N = 2$) this reduces to:

$$R_{ab} = R_a R_b \left(\frac{1}{R_a} + \frac{1}{R_b} \right) = \frac{R_a R_b (R_a + R_b)}{R_a R_b} = R_a + R_b$$

For a dangling resistor ($N = 1$) it results in the elimination of the resistor because $\binom{1}{2} = 0$.

Source transformation

A generator with an internal impedance (ie non-ideal generator) can be represented as either an ideal voltage generator or an ideal current generator plus the impedance. These two forms are equivalent and the transformations are given below. If the two networks are equivalent with respect to terminals ab, then V and I must be identical for both networks. Thus,

$$V_s = R I_s \text{ or } I_s = \frac{V_s}{R}$$

- Norton's theorem states that any two-terminal network can be reduced to an ideal current generator and a parallel impedance.
- Thévenin's theorem states that any two-terminal network can be reduced to an ideal voltage generator plus a series impedance.

Simple networks

Some very simple networks can be analysed without the need to apply the more systematic approaches.

Voltage division of series components

Consider n impedances that are connected in **series**. The voltage V_i across any impedance Z_i is

$$V_i = Z_i I = \left(\frac{Z_i}{Z_1 + Z_2 + \cdots + Z_n} \right) V$$

Current division of parallel components

Consider n impedances that are connected in **parallel**. The current I_i through any impedance Z_i is

$$I_i = \left(\frac{\left(\frac{1}{Z_i} \right)}{\left(\frac{1}{Z_1} \right) + \left(\frac{1}{Z_2} \right) + \cdots + \left(\frac{1}{Z_n} \right)} \right) I$$

for $i = 1, 2, ..., n.$

Special case: Current division of two parallel components

$$I_1 = \left(\frac{Z_2}{Z_1 + Z_2} \right) I$$

$$I_2 = \left(\frac{Z_1}{Z_1 + Z_2} \right) I$$

Nodal analysis

1. Label all **nodes** in the circuit. Arbitrarily select any node as reference.

2. Define a voltage variable from every remaining node to the reference. These voltage variables must be defined as voltage rises with respect to the reference node.

3. Write a KCL equation for every node except the reference.

4. Solve the resulting system of equations.

Mesh analysis

Mesh — a loop that does not contain an inner loop.

1. Count the number of "window panes" in the circuit. Assign a mesh current to each window pane.

2. Write a KVL equation for every mesh whose current is unknown.

3. Solve the resulting equations

Superposition

In this method, the effect of each generator in turn is calculated. All the generators other than the one being considered are removed; either short-circuited in the case of voltage generators, or open circuited in the case of current generators. The total current through, or the total voltage across, a particular branch is then calculated by summing all the individual currents or voltages.

There is an underlying assumption to this method that the total current or voltage is a linear superposition of its parts. The method cannot, therefore, be used if non-linear components are present. Note that mesh analysis and node analysis also implicitly use superposition so these too, are only applicable to linear circuits.

Choice of method

Choice of method[2] is to some extent a matter of taste. If the network is particularly simple or only a specific current or voltage is required then ad-hoc application of some simple equivalent circuits may yield the answer without recourse to the more systematic methods.

- Superposition is possibly the most conceptually simple method but rapidly leads to a large number of equations and messy impedance combinations as the network becomes larger.
- Nodal analysis: The number of voltage variables, and hence simultaneous equations to solve, equals the number of nodes minus one. Every voltage source connected to the reference node reduces the number of unknowns (and equations) by one. Nodal analysis is thus best for voltage sources.
- Mesh analysis: The number of current variables, and hence simultaneous equations to solve, equals the number of meshes. Every current source in a mesh reduces the number of unknowns by one. Mesh analysis is thus best for current sources. Mesh analysis, however, cannot be used with networks which cannot be drawn as a planar network, that is, with no crossing components.[3]

Transfer function

A transfer function expresses the relationship between an input and an output of a network. For resistive networks, this will always be a simple real number or an expression which boils down to a real number. Resistive networks are represented by a system of simultaneous algebraic equations. However in the general case of linear networks, the network is represented by a system of simultaneous linear differential equations. In network analysis, rather than use the differential equations directly, it is usual practice to carry out a Laplace transform on them first and then express the result in terms of the Laplace parameter s, which in general is complex. This is described as working in the s-domain. Working with the equations directly would be described as working in the time (or t) domain because the results would be expressed as time varying quantities. The Laplace transform is the mathematical method of transforming between the s-domain and the t-domain.

This approach is standard in control theory and is useful for determining stability of a system, for instance, in an amplifier with feedback.

Two terminal component transfer functions

For two terminal components the transfer function, otherwise called the constitutive equation, is the relationship between the current input to the device and the resulting voltage across it. The transfer function, Z(s), will thus have units of impedance - ohms. For the three passive components found in electrical networks, the transfer functions are;

Resistor $Z(s) = R$

Inductor $Z(s) = sL$

Capacitor $Z(s) = \dfrac{1}{sC}$

For a network to which only steady ac signals are applied, s is replaced with $j\omega$ and the more familiar values from ac network theory result.

$$\begin{aligned} \text{Resistor} && Z(j\omega) &= R \\ \text{Inductor} && Z(j\omega) &= j\omega L \\ \text{Capacitor} && Z(j\omega) &= \frac{1}{j\omega C} \end{aligned}$$

Finally, for a network to which only steady dc is applied, s is replaced with zero and dc network theory applies.

$$\begin{aligned} \text{Resistor} && Z &= R \\ \text{Inductor} && Z &= 0 \\ \text{Capacitor} && Z &= \infty \end{aligned}$$

Two port network transfer function

Transfer functions, in general, in control theory are given the symbol H(s). Most commonly in electronics, transfer function is defined as the ratio of output voltage to input voltage and given the symbol A(s), or more commonly (because analysis is invariably done in terms of sine wave response), A(jω), so that;

$$A(j\omega) = \frac{V_o}{V_i}$$

The A standing for attenuation, or amplification, depending on context. In general, this will be a complex function of jω, which can be derived from an analysis of the impedances in the network and their individual transfer functions. Sometimes the analyst is only interested in the magnitude of the gain and not the phase angle. In this case the complex numbers can be eliminated from the transfer function and it might then be written as;

$$A(\omega) = \left| \frac{V_o}{V_i} \right|$$

Two port parameters

The concept of a two-port network can be useful in network analysis as a black box approach to analysis. The behaviour of the two-port network in a larger network can be entirely characterised without necessarily stating anything about the internal structure. However, to do this it is necessary to have more information than just the A(jω) described above. It can be shown that four such parameters are required to fully characterise the two-port network. These could be the forward transfer function, the input impedance, the reverse transfer function (ie, the voltage appearing at the input when a voltage is applied to the output) and the output impedance. There are many others (see the main article for a full listing), one of these expresses all four parameters as impedances. It is usual to express the four parameters as a matrix;

$$\begin{bmatrix} V_1 \\ V_0 \end{bmatrix} = \begin{bmatrix} z(j\omega)_{11} & z(j\omega)_{12} \\ z(j\omega)_{21} & z(j\omega)_{22} \end{bmatrix} \begin{bmatrix} I_1 \\ I_0 \end{bmatrix}$$

The matrix may be abbreviated to a representative element;

$$[z(j\omega)] \text{ or just } [z]$$

These concepts are capable of being extended to networks of more than two ports. However, this is rarely done in reality as in many practical cases ports are considered either purely input or purely output. If reverse direction transfer functions are ignored, a multi-port network can always be decomposed into a number of two-port networks.

Distributed components

Where a network is composed of discrete components, analysis using two-port networks is a matter of choice, not essential. The network can always alternatively be analysed in terms of its individual component transfer functions. However, if a network contains distributed components, such as in the case of a transmission line, then it is not possible to analyse in terms of individual components since they do not exist. The most common approach to this is to model the line as a two-port network and characterise it using two-port parameters (or something equivalent to them). Another example of this technique is modelling the carriers crossing the base region in a high frequency transistor. The base region has to be modelled as distributed resistance and capacitance rather than lumped components.

Image analysis

Transmission lines and certain types of filter design use the image method to determine their transfer parameters. In this method, the behaviour of an infinitely long cascade connected chain of identical networks is considered. The input and output impedances and the forward and reverse transmission functions are then calculated for this infinitely long chain. Although, the theoretical values so obtained can never be exactly realised in practice, in many cases they serve as a very good approximation for the behaviour of a finite chain as long as it is not too short.

Non-linear networks

Most electronic designs are, in reality, non-linear. There is very little that does not include some semiconductor devices. These are invariably non-linear, the transfer function of an ideal semiconductor pn junction is given by the very non-linear relationship;

$$i = I_o(e^{\frac{v}{V_T}} - 1)$$

where;

- i and v are the instantaneous current and voltage.
- I_o is an arbitrary parameter called the reverse leakage current whose value depends on the construction of the device.
- V_T is a parameter proportional to temperature called the thermal voltage and equal to about 25mV at room temperature.

There are many other ways that non-linearity can appear in a network. All methods utilising linear superposition will fail when non-linear components are present. There are several options for dealing with non-linearity depending on the type of circuit and the information the analyst wishes to obtain.

Constitutive equations

The diode equation above is an example of a constitutive equation of the general form,

$$f(v, i) = 0$$

This can be thought of as a non-linear resistor. The corresponding constitutive equations for non-linear inductors and capacitors are respectively;

$$f(v, \varphi) = 0$$
$$f(v, q) = 0$$

where f is any arbitrary function, φ is the stored magnetic flux and q is the stored charge.

Existence, uniqueness and stability

An important consideration in non-linear analysis is the question of uniqueness. For a network composed of linear components there will always be one, and only one, unique solution for a given set of boundary conditions. This is not always the case in non-linear circuits. For instance, a linear resistor with a fixed voltage applied to it has only one solution for the current through it. On the other hand, the non-linear tunnel diode has up to three solutions for the current for a given voltage. That is, a particular solution for the current through the diode is not unique, there may be others, equally valid. In some cases there may not be a solution at all: the question of existence of solutions must be considered.

Another important consideration is the question of stability. A particular solution may exist, but it may not be stable, rapidly departing from that point at the slightest stimulation. It can be shown that a network that is absolutely stable for all conditions must have one, and only one, solution for each set of conditions.[4]

Methods

Boolean analysis of switching networks

A switching device is one where the non-linearity is utilised to produce two opposite states. CMOS devices in digital circuits, for instance, have their output connected to either the positive or the negative supply rail and are never found at anything in between except during a transient period when the device is actually switching. Here the non-linearity is designed to be extreme, and the analyst can actually take advantage of that fact. These kinds of networks can be analysed using Boolean algebra by assigning the two states ("on"/"off", "positive"/"negative" or whatever states are being used) to the boolean constants "0" and "1".

The transients are ignored in this analysis, along with any slight discrepancy between the actual state of the device and the nominal state assigned to a boolean value. For instance, boolean "1" may be assigned to the state of +5V. The output of the device may actually be +4.5V but the analyst still considers this to be boolean "1". Device manufacturers will usually specify a range of values in their data sheets that are to be considered undefined (ie the result will be unpredictable).

The transients are not entirely uninteresting to the analyst. The maximum rate of switching is determined by the speed of transition from one state to the other. Happily for the analyst, for many devices most of the transition occurs in the linear portion of the devices transfer function and linear analysis can be applied to obtain at least an approximate answer.

It is mathematically possible to derive boolean algebras which have more than two states. There is not too much use found for these in electronics, although three-state devices are passingly common.

Separation of bias and signal analyses

This technique is used where the operation of the circuit is to be essentially linear, but the devices used to implement it are non-linear. A transistor amplifier is an example of this kind of network. The essence of this technique is to separate the analysis in to two parts. Firstly, the dc biases are analysed using some non-linear method. This establishes the quiescent operating point of the circuit. Secondly, the small signal characteristics of the circuit are analysed using linear network analysis. Examples of methods that can be used for both these stages are given below.

Graphical method of dc analysis

In a great many circuit designs, the dc bias is fed to a non-linear component via a resistor (or possibly a network of resistors). Since resistors are linear components, it is particularly easy to determine the quiescent operating point of the non-linear device from a graph of its transfer function. The method is as follows: from linear network analysis the output transfer function (that is output voltage against output current) is calculated for the network of resistor(s) and the generator driving them. This will be a straight line and can readily be superimposed on the transfer function plot of the non-linear device. The point where the lines cross is the quiescent operating point.

Perhaps the easiest practical method is to calculate the (linear) network open circuit voltage and short circuit current and plot these on the transfer function of the non-linear device. The straight line joining these two point is the transfer function of the network.

In reality, the designer of the circuit would proceed in the reverse direction to that described. Starting from a plot provided in the manufacturers data sheet for the non-linear device, the designer would choose the desired operating point and then calculate the linear component values required to achieve it.

It is still possible to use this method if the device being biased has its bias fed through another device which is itself non-linear - a diode for instance. In this case however, the plot of the network transfer function onto the device being biased would no longer be a straight line and is consequently more tedious to do.

Small signal equivalent circuit

This method can be used where the deviation of the input and output signals in a network stay within a substantially linear portion of the non-linear devices transfer function, or else are so small that the curve of the transfer function can be considered linear. Under a set of these specific conditions, the non-linear device can be represented by an equivalent linear network. It must be remembered that this equivalent circuit is entirely notional and only valid for the small signal deviations. It is entirely inapplicable to the dc biasing of the device.

For a simple two-terminal device, the small signal equivalent circuit may be no more than two components. A resistance equal to the slope of the v/i curve at the operating point (called the dynamic resistance), and tangent to the curve. A generator, because this tangent will not, in general, pass through the origin. With more terminals, more complicated equivalent circuits are required.

A popular form of specifying the small signal equivalent circuit amongst transistor manufacturers is to use the two-port network parameters known as [h] parameters. These are a matrix of four parameters as with the [z] parameters but in the case of the [h] parameters they are a hybrid mixture of impedances, admittances, current gains and voltage gains. In this model the three terminal transistor is considered to be a two port network, one of its terminals being common to both ports. The [h] parameters are quite different depending on which terminal is chosen as the common one. The most important parameter for transistors is usually the forward current gain, h_{21}, in the common emitter configuration. This is designated h_{fe} on data sheets.

The small signal equivalent circuit in terms of two-port parameters leads to the concept of dependent generators. That is, the value of a voltage or current generator depends linearly on a voltage or current elsewhere in the circuit. For instance the [z] parameter model leads to dependent voltage generators as shown in this diagram;

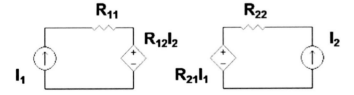

There will always be dependent generators in a two-port parameter equivalent circuit. This applies to the [h] parameters as well as to the [z] and any other kind. These dependencies must be preserved when developing the equations in a larger linear network analysis.

Piecewise linear method

In this method, the transfer function of the non-linear device is broken up into regions. Each of these regions is approximated by a straight line. Thus, the transfer function will be linear up to a particular point where there will be a discontinuity. Past this point the transfer function will again be linear but with a different slope.

A well known application of this method is the approximation of the transfer function of a pn junction diode. The actual transfer function of an ideal diode has been given at the top of this (non-linear) section. However, this formula is rarely used in network analysis, a piecewise approximation being used instead. It can be seen that the diode current rapidly diminishes to $-I_o$ as the voltage falls. This current, for most purposes, is so small it can be ignored. With increasing voltage, the current increases exponentially. The diode is modelled as an open circuit up to the knee of the exponential curve, then past this point as a resistor equal to the bulk resistance of the semiconducting material.

The commonly accepted values for the transition point voltage are 0.7V for silicon devices and 0.3V for germanium devices. An even simpler model of the diode, sometimes used in switching applications, is short circuit for forward voltages and open circuit for reverse voltages.

The model of a forward biased pn junction having an approximately constant 0.7V is also a much used approximation for transistor base-emitter junction voltage in amplifier design.

The piecewise method is similar to the small signal method in that linear network analysis techniques can only be applied if the signal stays within certain bounds. If the signal crosses a discontinuity point then the model is no longer valid for linear analysis purposes. The model does have the advantage over small signal however, in that it is equally applicable to signal and dc bias. These can therefore both be analysed in the same operations and will be linearly superimposable.

Time-varying components

In linear analysis, the components of the network are assumed to be unchanging, but in some circuits this does not apply, such as sweep oscillators, voltage controlled amplifiers, and variable equalisers. In many circumstances the change in component value is periodic. A non-linear component excited with a periodic signal, for instance, can be represented as periodically varying *linear* component. Sidney Darlington disclosed a method of analysing such periodic time varying circuits. He developed canonical circuit forms which are analogous to the canonical forms of Ronald Foster and Wilhelm Cauer used for analysing linear circuits.[5]

See also

- Bartlett's bisection theorem
- Circuit theory
- Equivalent impedance transforms
- Kirchhoff's circuit laws
- Mesh analysis
- Millman's Theorem
- Ohm's law
- Reciprocity theorem
- Resistive circuit
- Series and parallel circuits
- Tellegen's theorem
- Two-port network
- Wye-delta transform
- Symbolic circuit analysis

External links

- Circuit Analysis Techniques [6] — includes node/mesh analysis, superposition, and thevenin/norton transformation
- Nodal Analysis of Op Amp Circuits [7]
- Analysis of Resistive Circuits [8]
- Circuit Analysis Related Laws, Examples and Solutions [9]
- Solved problems in electrical circuits [10]

References

[1] Belevitch V (May 1962). "Summary of the history of circuit theory". *Proceedings of the IRE* **50** (5): 849. doi:10.1109/JRPROC.1962.288301. cites "IRE Standards on Circuits: Definitions of Terms for Linear Passive Reciprocal Time Invariant Networks, 1960". *Proceedings of the IRE* **48** (9): 1609. September 1960. doi:10.1109/JRPROC.1960.287676.to justify this definition.

Sidney Darlington Darlington S (1984). "A history of network synthesis and filter theory for circuits composed of resistors, inductors, and capacitors". *IEEE Trans. Circuits and Systems* **31** (1): 4.

follows Belevitch but notes there are now also many colloquial uses of "network".

[2] Nilsson, J W, Riedel, S A (2007). *Electric Circuits* (http://books.google.com/books?id=sxmM8RFL99wC&lpg=PA200&dq=isbn:0131989251&lr=&as_drrb_is=q&as_minm_is=0&as_miny_is=&as_maxm_is=0&as_maxy_is=&as_brr=0&pg=PA112#v=onepage&q=112&f=false) (8th ed.). Pearson Prentice Hall. pp. 112–113. ISBN 0-13-198925-1. .

[3] Nilsson, J W, Riedel, S A (2007). *Electric Circuits* (http://books.google.com/books?id=sxmM8RFL99wC&lpg=PA200&dq=isbn:0131989251&lr=&as_drrb_is=q&as_minm_is=0&as_miny_is=&as_maxm_is=0&as_maxy_is=&as_brr=0&pg=PA94#v=onepage&q=&f=false) (8th ed.). Pearson Prentice Hall. p. 94. ISBN 0-13-198925-1. .

[4] Ljiljana Trajković, "Nonlinear circuits", *The Electrical Engineering Handbook* (Ed: Wai-Kai Chen), pp.79-81, Academic Press, 2005 ISBN 0121709604

[5] Sidney Darlington, Irwin W. Sandberg, "Synthesis of two-port networks having periodically time-varying elements", US patent 3265973 (http://v3.espacenet.com/textdoc?DB=EPODOC&IDX=US3265973), issued 1966-08-09

Analytical expression

In mathematics, an **analytical expression** (or **expression in analytical form**) is a mathematical expression, constructed using well-known operations that lend themselves readily to calculation. As for closed-form expressions, the criteria are not precisely defined, but the class of expressions considered to be "analytical expressions" tends to be wider.

In particular, special functions such as the Bessel functions and the gamma function are usually allowed, and often so are infinite series and continued fractions. On the other hand, limits in general, and integrals in particular, are typically excluded.

Article Sources and Contributors

SNAP (software) *Source*: http://en.wikipedia.org/w/index.php?oldid=359961633 *Contributors*: Beniek, Fiftyquid, Frecklefoot, P100011011, Rogerbrent, 1 anonymous edits

Microsoft Windows *Source*: http://en.wikipedia.org/w/index.php?oldid=370756640 *Contributors*: -Majestic-, 03jmgibbens, 1(), 16@r, 1nt2, 2mcm, 2toy mora, 62.253.64.xxx, 67773732TYU, 68DANNY2, 9ms, A Raider Like Indiana, A gnome, A-giau, ACCOM2222, Abhishikt, AbsoluteFlatness, Academic Challenger, Acroterion, Adam Mirowski, Adamacious, Adamodell, Admin@pcrevs.com, Ae-a, Aeæ, Afro Article, Ageha Winds, Ahodacsek, Ahoerstemeier, Aidan W, Aido2002, Aihtdikh, AimalCool, Ajm81, Akamad, Akhristov, Akira-otomo, Aksi great, Albert0057, Aldie, Alegoo92, Alemily, Alfio, AlistairMcMillan, Allstarecho, Almafeta, Althepal, Am088, Amcfreely, Amrykid, Andre Engels, Andrevan, Andrewtechhelp, Andros 1337, Andy16666, Andyh2, Angeljon121, Ann Stouter, Anog, Anonymous Dissident, Anonymous56789, Antandrus, Anthall1991, Antimatter15, Antique Rose, Anville, Anþony, Aomarks, Aqair, Aranel, Arch dude, Archer3, Archivist, Arnoldkul, Arthena, Ashdurbat, AstroNomer, Astroview120mm, Aude, Audrius u, AussieLegend, AvantgardeMVC, Avenue, Avihut, Avocado27, Ayjay1545, Azrael Nightwalker, B, BNSF Man, BUzTeD, Badwolf2212, Bakery2k, Banes, Barrera marquez, Bartosz, Bbq man, Bbriggs1, Bdoserror, Beinsane, Ben-Zin, Benandorsqueaks, Benc, Berek, Bergsten, Betelgeuse, Bevo, Bhadani, Bibliomaniac15, Big Booger, BigCow, BillG, BillWSmithJr, Billyswong, Bimmerosx, Binsurf, Binzisimpsons, Bissinger, Blackanddarkness, Blackcats, Blakkandekka, Blaxthos, Bleakcomb, Blobglob, Blowdart, Blubberboy92, Blueforce4116, Bluestriker, Bo98, Bobo192, Bobwrit, Bogods, Boris Allen, BostonMA, Boylett, Brandizzi, Brandon Brown, Brian0918, BrianGo28, BrianRecchia, Brianski, Brisvegas, BrokenSegue, Bubba hotep, Buchanan-Hermit, Buddha24, Burntsauce, CRFWNY, Cacophony, Caffelice, Caltas, Camembert, Can't sleep, clown will eat me, Canadian-Bacon, Candamir, Candorwien, CanisRufus, Caper13, CaptainVindaloo, Casper2k3, Cayindra, Cbrown1023, Cburnett, Ceeon, Celestra, CesarB, Ceyockey, Cff12345, Cgnabod, Cgs, Charles Gaudette, Charles dye, Chazz, Chille, Chmpoure, Chocolatemilk94, Chowbok, Chris 73, Chris Pickett, Chris the speller, Christian List, Chriswoz, Ciao 90, CitronManden, Cityscape4, Cjcamilla, Cjordan93, ClockworkTroll, Cncccer, Codificate, Codyblevins, Coffee, Colin Hill, Cometstyles, Commander Keane, Computer boy2, Computerdan000, ConCompS, Coniosis, Conman23456, Conversion script, Coolcaesar, CoolingGibbon, Corporal clegg48, Cp111, Cpiral, Crazycomputers, Crazyromo, Crem23, Cremepuff222, Cristan, Crpietschmann, Cryptic, Cstanners, Ctbolt, Cuvtixo, Cvinoth, Cwolfsheep, Cyktsui, Cynical, Cyrius, D, D thadd, DHN, DOHC Holiday, DaDrumBum, DalekClock, Damian Yerrick, Dan D. Ric, Daniel5127, DanielRigal, Danny Beaudoin, DarkFalls, DarkHorizon, Darranc, Darremon, Darthnader37, Dasani, DataMatrix, Databases, Davelane, David Biddulph, David Gerard, David1409, Davidjk, Dcandeto, Dcolvin, Deanhowell123, Debackerl, Deeahbz, Dehumanizer, Delirium, Delldot, Deltabeignet, Demmy, Denniss, Derek Parnell, Deryck Chan, Dethomas, Deus2, Dieboybun, Diegogrez, Digita, DigitalLife, Dimre01, Dina, Dinjired, DinosaursLoveExistence, Disorganisation Man, Dj789, Djegan, Djhybrid117, Djmasala, Dmerrill, DmitryKo, Dog1818, Dojarca, Dolphinn, Downloaddude1258, Dp462090, Dragar Gt, Dragon 280, DragonflySixtyseven, Dragonhelmuk, Drini, Dstln, Dtech, Dudesleeper, Dungodung, Dust Filter, Dustin gayler, Dwheeler, Dysprosia, Dzubint, EH74DK, Eagleal, EatMyShortz, Ed g2s, Edgar181, Edgarde, EdgeOfEpsilon, Eelamstylez77, Eggsacute, Egil, El Dominio, Elassint, Eliotwiki, ElliotAdderton, Ellmist, Elm-39, Eloquence, Emacsuser, Enco1984, Enigmaaaaa, Enno, Enochlau, Ente75, Ergosteur, Esanchez7587, Escape Orbit, Evice, Evil Monkey, Evil saltine, Evosoho, Ewlyahoocom, Exodite, F.A.I.T.H.L.E.S.S, F80, Faisal.akeel, Faithlessthewonderboy, Falco McCloud, Fantasy, Faradayplank, FatalError, Fatjoe151, FayssalF, Fbv65edel, Fdp, Felipe Aira, Ferkelparade, Ffx, Fiskegalen92, Fitzebwoy, Fiver2552, Flamurai, Flanakin, Flash200, FleetCommand, Flying Bishop, FlyingPenguins, Foo1995, Fowl2, FrancoGG, Frap, Fraslet, Freakofnurture, Frecklefoot, Fred Bradstadt, Frederik.Questier, FreeKresge, Freeeekyyy, Frenchman113, FreplySpang, FrozenPurpleCube, Frozenport, Fuck You, Funandtrvl, Furrykef, Fuzheado, GDonato, GNUtoo, GSK, Gadfium, Gaius Cornelius, Galactor213, Galoubet, Galwhaa, GamerXp, Gamerzworld, Gaming&Computing, Ganeshotaku, Ganfon, Gang65, Gaodifan, Gardar Rurak, Gary King, Gary Kirk, Gazpacho, Geek45, Geoffspear, George Adam Horváth, Georgia guy, Geraki, Gerbrant, Ghettoblaster, Gilbertogm, Gilliam, Glen, Gnepets, Goatasaur, Gogo Dodo, Goldom, Googler459, Googlesucks56789, Gosub, Graham87, GrandPoohBah, Grayshi, Grin, Grm wnr, Groggy Dice, Gronky, Grunt, Gscshoyru, Gtdp, Gunnar Guðvarðarson, Gustyfalcon, Guy Harris, Guyjohnston, Haakon, Haeleth, Hahafatpeople, Hairchrm, Hall Monitor, Halsteadk, Hammersoft, Happenstance, Harryboyles, Haseo9999, Hbomb phd mom, Hdt83, Heapchk, Hebrides, Helixblue, Hello32020, Hendrixski, Henry W. Schmitt, HereToHelp, Hirosho, Holbred, Howardjp, Hungupbg, Hurtstotalktoyou, Husky, Hydr, Hypnoticcyst, I8189720, IGod, ILOVELOL32, IMSoP, IXella007, Iain99, Ian Pitchford, Ianjones50, Illegal Operation, Illyria05, Ilya, IlyaHaykinson, Ilyanep, Indefatigable, Indon, Injust, Interframe, Ioprwe, Ipodsocool, Iridescent, ItsProgrammable, Ivan Pozdeev, Ixfd64, J Di, JCarriker, JIP, JLaTondre, JWSchmidt, JYOuyang, JYolkowski, Jacob Hnri 5, JacquesStrap, Jaericho, Jake Wasdin, James Michael 1, Jamieostrich, Jan Hofmann, Jauerback, Jaxl, Jcbparry, Jcurtin, Jdlowery, Jdm64, Jeffwang16, Jeremy Visser, JeremyA, Jerryseinfeld, Jerrysmp, Jesse Viviano, Jesus5555, Jesus764, Jesuss, JettaMann, Jevel66, Jiffy, Jigs41793, Jimmi Hugh, Jimothytrotter, Jimthing, Jiy, Jketola, Jkonline, Jmath666, Jmjglick, Jmoynihan08hm77, JoJan, JoThousand, Joanjoc, JoanneB, Joejoejo, Joffeloff, Johann Wolfgang, John, John Ericson, John Goettle, JohnOwens, Johnclow13, Johnleemk, Johnmc, Johnuniq, Jojit fb, Jon vs, JonasL, Jonatan Swift, Jondel, Jonghyunchung, Jopxton, Jordan015, Josh the Nerd, Joshua Issac, JoshuaArgent, Joyous!, Jpoke89, Jrcure, Jsmethers, Jtc, Ju66l3r, JuJube, JuanC08, Julian Mendez, Jumbo Snails, Justanother, Jyoz, Kakomu, Kar.ma, Karimarie, Karnesky, Kaycubs, Kaysov, Kbh3rd, Kbolino, Kelly Martin, Kesla, Kevinkor2, Keyser Söze, Khym Chanur, Kierenj, Kigali1, KingpinE7, Kinneyboy90, Kipholbeck, Kissmeplease, Kjhonsa, Kkm010, Klingoncowboy4, KnowledgeOfSelf, Knutux, Kohlmalo, Kolonuk, Korossyl, Kozuch, KrakatoaKatie, Krawi, Kungfuadam, Kungming2, Kurieeto, Kwen, La goutte de pluie, Lacrimosus, Lahiru k, Lantay77, Larry laptop, Lbs6380, Lcarsdata, Lead$peaker, Leandrod, Lectonar, LeeHunter, Leif, Leithp, LeoNomis, Letdorf, Leuko, Liberty Miller, Lightmouse, Linear88, Linuxbeak, Linuxerist, LionKimbro, Llalala, Localzuk, Lonaowna, LonelyBeacon, Lookslíketrent, Lou.weird, Lowellian, Luce007, Luk, Lumpbucket, Luna Santin, Lupin, M Johnson, MADCastro2012, MCC, MER-C, MERC, MJGR, MK8, MMMEEE, MZMcBride, Ma8thew, Mac, MacGeekGuy, Madcow 93, Maester mensch, Mailer diablo, Malo, Man123123, Marceki111, Marcok, Mark, Mark85296341, MarkGallagher, MarkSpearmint, Markhurd, Markie2, Martarius, Martyx, Marudubshinki, Marx Gomes, Marysunshine, Massysett, MasterCole, Mastershake86, Mathwizxp, Matt Crypto, Mattarata, Mav, Max Schwarz, Maxim Masiutin, Maximus Rex, McLovin34, Mcwatson, Meelar, MehranVB, Mephiles602, Metalim, Methanegas, Metz2000, Mguy77, Mgw854, Michael Angelkovich, Michael Ray, Michaeldadmum, Michaelpremsrirat, Midgrid, Midkay, Mike4ty4, MikeZuniga, Mild Bill Hiccup, Milfman, Minesweeper, MinorItem, Mithent, Mjpieters, Mkdw, Mlscdi, Mmoll21m, Mms, Mo0, Modster, Monedula, MontyB, Moonknightus, Moonridersaregay, Moonwolf14, Mr Bartels, Mr. Lefty, Mr. XYZ, Mrdelayer, Ms2ger, Mugunth Kumar, Mulad, Mushroom, Mvmarier, Mwtoews, Mxn, Myanw, Nachmore, Naddy, Naltrexone, Nanshu, NapoliRoma, Nathan nfm, Nathanlilienthal13, Neelchauhan, Neo2256, NewGuy4, Nick2253, Nimc, Nintendog master 54, Nishkid64, Nixdorf, Njan, Nmnmnm, Noypi380, Nukleartoaster, Nurg, O, Odd bloke, Off!, Okwestern, OlEnglish, Olioster, Ollie the Magic Skater, Omicronpersei8, Ondrejsv, Oneupthextraman, Opagecrtr, Opelio, OregonD00d, Oscarthecat, Ost316, OtherPerson, OwenX, Oxymoron83, Ozherb, PPGMD, Packard Bell Legend, Padsquad43, Pakaran, Patrick, Patrickweeks007, Patrolman89, Paul Cyr, Paul Stansifer, Paulfp, Pavel Vozenilek, Persian Poet Gal, Petaluma Paranormal, Peter Grey, Peteturtle, Petrwiki, Peyman4u, Peyre, Pgiii, Pgk, Phanton, Phil Sandifer, Philip Trueman, Pigman, Pile0nades, Pinikas, Piratesmack, Plugwash, Pokyrek, Poor Yorick, Poweroid, Prolog, Propound, Pschulz01, PsyMar, Pursey, QUAZWRATH, Qudder, Quinsareth, Qwerty124gg, Qwitchibo, Qxl32, Qxz, RB972, RN, RTC, RadioActive, Radon210, Raja99, Ramanpotential, RandomP, Rasmasyean, Rbuj, Rchamberlain, Rcmouse1010, Rd syringe, Rderijcke, Rdsmith4, Reallikeunreal, Rebecca, Rebroad, Red Dalek, Red Director, RedKlonoa, RedXII, Redvers, Reilly, Reisio, Remember the dot, Repetition, Resplendent, RevolverOcelotX, Rhesusmonkeyboy, Rhobite, Rhtc, Rich Farmbrough, Richard Lotspard, Richard626, Ricjl, RickK, Riluve, Rjecina, Rjwilmsi, Rlevse, Roadrunnah, Robartin, Robbie940, Robert Buzink, Robert H, Robert Xia, RobertG, Robertd, Robinhw, Rocastelo, Rocket71048576, Rockymountains, Rodeo90, Roketjack, RolandH, Ronark, Rsantmann, Rsm99833, Running, Rursus, Rutherfordjigsaw, Ruud Koot, Rwwww, Ryan Postlethwaite, Ryan t moua, S0aasdf2sf, SF007, SHARD, SHeumann, SNIyer12, ST47, SYSS Mouse, Sam Hocevar, Samuel, Samuel Blanning, Samvscat, Sango123, Sasquatch, Sauronjim, Scepia, SchmuckyTheCat, SchuminWeb, Science4sail, Scientus, Scifiintel, Sciurinæ, Scorpiona, Scottymoze, Scriberius, Scuiqui fox, SeanMack, Sebmathews, Sebrat, Secretlondon, Secretmessages, Selfdiscipline, Selivanow, September 11 terrorist, Sethoeph, Sfan00 IMG, Shakumafu, Shandris, Shanes, Shashank Shekhar, Shelmac, Shibboleth, Shinjiman, Shnout, Sigma 7, Sigmundpetersen, Sikon, Silvergoat, SimonEast, SimonP, SimonTrew, Simxp, SirGrant, Siroxo, Sjakkalle, Sjorford, Skirks, Skiwi, Skyeap, Slashuer, Slathering, Sleepeeg3, Slipknotmetal, Smokizzy, SmoothNikola, Smurfy, Smyth, Snaxe920, Snoyes, SoSaysChappy, Solphusion, Somaditya, Somebody in the WWW, Soumyasch, Southpark20, Spe88, Spear of fire, Specter01010, SpeedyGonsales, Spencerperry, Sperling, Spliced, Spookfish, Spug, Srnelson, Ssd, Starionwolf, Steel, StephenH, Stephenchou0722, SteveRwanda, Stevenh123, Stevietheman, Stilroc, Stino v, Stonda, StuIsCool, StuThomas, Supers, Supremeknowledge, Suruena, SusanLesch, Susvolans, Swabjob, Sweetback, Swollib, Swotboy2000, SyntaxError55, Syrthiss, Szhang21, TAG.Odessa, TJ Spyke, Ta bu shi da yu, Tacvek, Tadas12, TakuyaMurata, Tangotango, Tannin, Tarashav, Tawker, Teamcritical, Tech2blog, Techman224, Techmdrn, Template namespace initialisation script, Tepidpond, Terence, TerrenceandPhillip, Thaek, Thalakan, Thavian, The Colclough, The Disco Times, The Epopt, The Fish, The Geneticist, The Rambling Man, The wub, TheChrisD, TheDoober, TheKMan, TheNewPhobia, ThePointblank, Thealexweb, Theazman1, Thegreenj, Thetehror, Thewallowmaker, Thewikipedian, Thingg, Think outside the box, This, that and the other, Thisisntfake1, Thomas H. Larsen, Thompson.matthew, Thorpe, Throup, Thu, Thumperward, TiCPU, Tiggerjay, TimR, Timmeh, Timwi, Tinton5, ToasterOS, Tomcage9, Tomi Undergallows, Tommy Irianto, Tompagenet, Tonsofpcs, Tony1, Tothwolf, Towel401, Towsonu2003, Toyotaboy95, Treekids, Tregoweth, TrekMaster, Trevor MacInnis, Tripacer99, Trivialist, Trusilver, Tsunaminoai, Ttwaring, TubularWorld, TuneyLoon, Turionaltec, TuukkaH, Twernt, Tyomitch, Tyraios, UMC2, Uli, Ultimus, Umofomia, Unimaginative Username, Unknownperson1234, Uriel8, Utcursch, Vahid83, Vbrtrmn, Vedek Dukat, Vegaswikian, Vincent.premysler, Vontafeijos, Wackymacs, Walter Görlitz, WalterGR, Wanderson9, Wangmike, Wapcaplet, Warlordwolf, Warren, Wengier, Werdan7, Werideatdusk33, Whiteford8, Whkoh, Widefox, Wiki alf, Wiki fanatic, WikiBone, WikiFew, WikiMan44, Wikinger, WikipedianMarlith, Wikiwaka101, Windowsknowitall@msn.com, WindowzRULZlolZ, Windsok, Wknight94, Wlklpedla is meant to be vandalized, Wmahan, Wmplayer, Wow1000, Wykis, X1987x, XJamRastafire, Xation, Xelgen, Xeysz, Xgmx, Ximian99, Xlation, Xmachina, Xp54321, Xpclient, XrXeJoeXaXpXeXr, Xtreme racer, Xtremerandomness, YUL89YYZ, Yama, Yamamoto Ichiro, Yamla, Yasirniazkhan, Yeeshenhao, Yergizmo, Ynhockey, Yousifnet, Yuckfoo, Yuhong, Z.E.R.O., Z98, ZFU738, Zakfleming, Zapvet, Zeeboid, Zepheus, Zntrip, Zondor, Zoney, Zundark, , 乌尔奇奥拉, 每日飞龙, 1494 anonymous edits

Analog circuits *Source*: http://en.wikipedia.org/w/index.php?oldid=84306235 *Contributors*: Afed, Alan Liefting, Alf Boggis, AndrewHowse, Audioamp, Binksternet, Bobo192, Brews ohare, Casper2k3, Cburnett, Corpx, Derfee, Dicklyon, Edward Z. Yang, Edwardkwt, Etphonehome, Evanreyes, Fourohfour, Garett Long, George Burgess, GyroMagician, Hence Jewish Anderstein, Heron, JDPhD, Jaganath, Jp314159, Jpbowen, Kerowyn, Light current, Lindosland, Masgatotkaca, Mbell, Mdd4696, Mhowkins, Micoru, Moqueur roux, Nestea Zen, Neurogeek, Oldmountains, Pearle, Pgavin, RJFJR, Radagast83, SCEhardt, Sanguinity, Simetrical, Sleigh, Stemonitis, Steven Zhang, TheParanoidOne, Timl2k4, Tresiden, Wtshymanski, 76 anonymous edits

Linear *Source*: http://en.wikipedia.org/w/index.php?oldid=370635462 *Contributors*: 16@r, Alan Liefting, Alansohn, Algebraist, Altenmann, Andre Engels, Army1987, Astroview120mm, AxelBoldt, Bamadude, Bernard François, Bobo192, Bogdangiusca, Bonadea, Bwashed, CRGreathouse, Can't sleep, clown will eat me, Capricorn42, Charles Matthews, Clemmy, Colonies Chris, Complexica, CyborgTosser, Cyp, DVD R W, Darkdan, Davidovic, Dcljr, Discospinster, DrJos, Drz, Dystopos, EPO, Epbr123, Everyking, False vacuum, Ffaarr, Fners, Fredrik, Furry Roadkill, Fuzzbox, Giftlite, Glich, Goystein, Grafen, Gregbard, Histrion, Hyacinth, Icestorm815, Insanity Incarnate, Karada, Kathryn NicDhàna, Kbk, Kendalfong, Kl4m, Levineps, Linas, Longhair, MC10, Maksim-e, Malerin, Master on EN, Mattpickman, Melchoir, Michael Hardy, Michael Slone, Mikeblas, Mikiemike, Minimiscience, Moomoomoo, NawlinWiki, Nirion, Nixdorf, Oddity-, Oleg Alexandrov, Oliver Pereira, Oodymex, PFFT!2007, PSHT!2008, PV=nRT, Paolo.dL, Patrick, Persian Poet Gal, Purplefeltangel, PuzzletChung, R'n'B, RDBury, Razorflame, Rbj, Rettetast,

Roadrunner, Rsepahi, Rtdrury, Sam Hocevar, Science4sail, Scwlong, SilkTork, Silly rabbit, Slakr, Sligocki, Smoken Flames, Steven J. Anderson, Stevenj, Stevertigo, Stomme, Tarquin, The Anome, The Thing That Should Not Be, The stuart, Theaterfreak64, Thingg, Tohd8BohaithuGh1, Tone, Torchwooddoctor, Traxs7, Trovatore, Wimt, ZAB, Zootm, 168 anonymous edits

Schematic capture Source: http://en.wikipedia.org/w/index.php?oldid=368217263 Contributors: Abdull, Altenmann, Chimpex, Chter, DavidCary, Dcfleck, Duaneb, East718, Geni, Glrx, Hooperbloob, IlijaKovacevic, InterruptorJones, Kglavin, Lmjohnson, Microfrost, Omegatron, Poppafuze, Rclocher3, Rhinotail, Rundquist, S Roper, Scottfisher, Spinningspark, Stasruev, Strubin, Thewoost, Tournesol, Youssefsan, 36 anonymous edits

SapWin Source: http://en.wikipedia.org/w/index.php?oldid=359962399 Contributors: Beniek, Fiftyquid, Free Software Knight, Johnpacklambert, Rogerbrent, Sliker Hawk, 3 anonymous edits

Symbolic Circuit Analysis Source: http://en.wikipedia.org/w/index.php?oldid=360549898 Contributors: Beniek, Malcolma, Mandarax, Mild Bill Hiccup, Rich Farmbrough, Rpyle731, Spinningspark

Laplace Source: http://en.wikipedia.org/w/index.php?oldid=284811269 Contributors: 16@r, 213.253.39.xxx, 3mta3, 5 albert square, Ac1201, Adam McMaster, Ahoerstemeier, Ajb, Alfio, Amicon, Amnrahimian, Andre Engels, Andres, Angela, AnonMoos, Arcadia616, Asperal, Asyndeton, AtticusX, Attilios, AugPi, Bachrach44, Bemoeial, Ben-Zin, Bender235, BerndGehrmann, Bkonrad, Blueboy814, Bracodbk, Bsskchaitanya, Bubba73, C.Fred, Can't sleep, clown will eat me, Caroldermoid, Charles Matthews, Chicheley, Chris Hardy, Chris the speller, ChrisfromHouston, Courcelles, Cozy, CrocodileMile, Curps, Cutler, Cyan, D6, DJ Clayworth, Dadude3320, Dchristle, Deb, Den fjättrade ankan, Dispersion, Doctorsundar, Docu, Dv82matt, ERcheck, Eeekster, Electron9, Ellywa, Elsweyn, Elysnoss, Emerson7, Eric Kvaalen, Everyking, Francis Schonken, Gaara144, Gadfium, Gauss, Geni, GeoGreg, Giftlite, Gliese876, Gmaxwell, Goochelaar, GraemeL, Graham87, GregorB, Haham hanuka, Hannoscholtz, HappyApple, Hektor, Hemmingsen, Hongooi, Hqb, Husond, Indiedude, J.delanoy, J04n, JASpencer, Jaerik, Jamesmorrison, Jaredwf, Jaytan, Jmu2108, Johan1298, John, Johnbibby, Jojit fb, Joseph Solis in Australia, Jugbo, Julesd, Jumbuck, Jusdafax, Knutux, Kostisl, Kraxler, LarryB55, Lexor, LilHelpa, Lova Falk, Lradrama, Lucidish, Lunarian, Lupo, Lzur, Mackensen, Maestlin, Maghnus, Manop, Marcus2, Markus Poessel, MartinHarper, Mashford, Melsaran, Metasquares, Michael Hardy, Mike Rosoft, Mild Bill Hiccup, Mion, Mitteldorf, Mneideng, Monegasque, Mpatel, Mschlindwein, NBeale, NeueWelt, Neutrality, New World Man, Nicolaennio, Nixdorf, Nk, Oleg Alexandrov, Olivier, Paine Ellsworth, Palnot, Paolo.dL, Paul August, PaulGarner, PdDemeter, Pinincc65, Pizza1512, Pmanderson, Pohick2, Pointqwert, Pred, Promus Kaa, Psients, Ptranouez, Punstar, QueenAdelaide, Quess, QuiteUnusual, Qwfp, RJHall, RS1900, Randombluе, Rbj, Rdanneskjold, Renatops, Riisikuppi, Robma, Rory096, SMStigler, Sadi Carnot, Sam Hocevar, Samuel, Santa Sangre, Schlier22, SchuminWeb, ScienceApologist, SevereTireDamage, SimonTrew, SlamDiego, Snoyes, StephenFerg, Studerby, Stwalkerster, Sublium, TangoTheory, Tarotcards, TedE, Terry0051, The Thing That Should Not Be, Themerejoy, Tiddly Tom, Tomas e, Tomixdf, Tpbradbury, Tt 225, Uksam88, Unara, Urhixidur, Utcursch, UtilityIsKing, Vojvodaen, Vsmith, WolfmanSF, XJamRastafire, XM, Zoicon5, 408 anonymous edits

C++ Source: http://en.wikipedia.org/w/index.php?oldid=371253992 Contributors: -Barry-, 12.21.224.xxx, 223ankher, 4jobs, 4th-otaku, 7DaysForgotten, @modi, A D Monroe III, A.A.Graff, AIOS, ALOTOFTOMATOES, AMackenzie, AThing, ATren, Aandu, Abdull, Abi79, Adam12901, Addihockey10, Adi211095, Adorno rocks, Ae-a, Aesopos, Agasta, AgentFriday, Ahmadmashhour, Ahoerstemeier, Ahy1, Akeegazooka, Akersmc, Akhristov, Akihabara, Akuyume, Alan D, AlbertCahalan, AlecSchueler, Aleenf1, AlexKarpman, Alexf, Alexius08, Alexkon, Alfio, Alhoori, Aliekens, AlistairMcMillan, Allstarecho, AltiusBimm, Alxeedo, AnAccount2, AnOddName, Andante1980, Andre Engels, Andreaskem, Andrew Delong, Andrew1, AndrewHowse, AndrewKepert, Andyluciano, AngelOfSadness, Angela, Anoko moonlight, Anonymous Dissident, Antandrus, Aparna.amar.patil, Apexofservice, Arabic Pilot, Aragorn2, Arcadie, Arctic.gnome, Ardonik, Asimzb, Atjesse, Atlant, Auntof6, Austin Hair, Autopilot, Avoran, Axecution, AxelBoldt, BMW Z3, Baa, Babija, Babjisit, Bahram.zahir, Barek, Baronnet, Bart133, Bartosz, Bdragon, Belem tower, BenFrantzDale, Benhocking, Bento00, Beowulf king, Bevo, Beyondthislife, Bfzhao, Biblioth3que, Bigk105, Bill gates69, Bineet, Bkil, Blaisorblade, Bluemoose, Bluezy, Bobazoid, Bobblewik, Bobo192, Bobthebill, Bodkinator, Boffob, Boing! said Zebedee, Bomarrow1, Bongwarrior, Booklegger, Bosoko, Bovineone, Brion VIBBER, Btx40, C Labombard, C++ Template, C.Fred, CALR, CIreland, CPMcE, CRGreathouse, CWY2190, Caesura, Caiaffa, Callek, Caltas, Can't sleep, clown will eat me, CanisRufus, Cap'n Refsmmat, Capi crimm, CapitalR, Capricorn42, Captainhampton, Carabinieri, Carbon-sieve, Catgut, Cathack, CecilWard, Cedars, CesarB, Cetinsert, Cfeet77, Cflm001, Cgranade, Chaos5023, CharlotteWebb, Chealer, Chocolateboy, Chrisandtaund, Christian List, Chuq, Ckburke, Cleared as filed, Closedmouth, Clsdennis2007, Cometstyles, Comperr, Conversion script, Coolwanglu, Coosbane, Coq Rouge, CordeliaNaismith, Corrector7007, Corti, Cowsnatcher27, Craig Stuntz, Cromate, Csmaster2005, Ctu2485, Cubbi, Curps, Cwitty, Cybercobra, Cyclonenim, Cyde, CyrilleDunant, Cyrius, DAGwyn, DJ Clayworth, DVD R W, Dallison999, Damian Yerrick, Damien.c.sadler, Dan Brown123, Dan100, Danakil, Daniel Earwicker, Daniel.Cardenas, DanielNuyu, Dario D., DarkHorizon, Derek Ross, DerylK, Dan-DevSolar, DevastatorIIC, Dibash, Diego pmc, Discospinster, Dlae, Dfkja3skj, Dmharvey, Dogcow, DominicConnor, DonelleDer, Donhalcon, Doofenschmirtzevilinc, DoubleRing, Doug Bell, Dougjih, Doulos Christos, Dragon, Drewcifer3000, Drmgrvy, DyInuge, Dysprosia, E Wing, ESkog, Eagleal, Eark Martin, EartMyShortz, Ebeisher, Eco84, Ecstatickid, Ed Brey, Edward F, Eebster the great, Eelis.net, Ehn, Elliskev, Elysdir, Enarsee, EncMH, Enerjazzer, Engineerbeing, Eric119, ErikHaugen, Esanchez7587, Esben, Esmitts, Esrogs, EternalAscent08, Ethan, EvanED, Evice, Evil Monkey, Ewok18, Excirial, FW4NK, Fa2sA, Facorread, Faithlessthewonderboy, Faizni, Falcon300000, Fanf, Fashionslide, FatalError, Favonian, Fistboy, Fizzackerly, Flaminganticchimp, Flash200, Flewis, Flex, Flyingprogrammer, FrancoGG, Freakofnurture, Freckleloot, Free Software Knight, Freshereez, Fritzpoll, Ftbhrygvn, Furby100, Furrykef, Fuzzbyte, GLari, Gaul, Gauss, Geooharee, Gene.thomas, Gengiskanhg, Giftlite, Gil mo, Gildos, Gilgamesh, Gimili2, Gimme danger, Gmcfoley, God Of All, Gogo Dodo, GoodSirJava, Graue, Greatdebtor, GregorB, Gremagor, Grenavitar, Grey GosHawk, Grigor The Ox, Gsonnenf, Gusmoe, Gwern, Gwjames, Hairy Dude, Hakkinen, HappyCamper, Harald Hansen, Harinisanthosh, Harryboyles, HebrewHammerTime, HeikoEvermann, Hemanshu, HenryLi, Herorev, Hervegirod, Hetar, Hgfernan, HideandLeek, Hihahiha474, Hiraku.n, Hmains, Hobartimus, Hogman500, Horselover Frost, Hoss7994, Hu, Hu12, Husond, Hyad, Hyperfusion, I already forgot, IsoLoveHer, Iamninja91, Ibroadfo, Imc, Immunize, InShanece, Innocent, Insanity Incarnate, Intangir, Iphoneorange, Iridescence, Iridescent, Irish Souffle, Ironholds, Isaacl, Ixfd64, J Casanova, J Di, J-A-V-A, J.delanoy, JForget, JNighthawk, Jackelfive, Jafet, Jaredwf, Jatos, Javiercastillo73, Javierito92, Jawed, Jayaram ganapathy, Jdent29, Jdowland, Jeff G., JeffTL, Jeltz, Jerry teps, Jerryobject, Jesma, Jesse Viviano, Jesse W, Jgamer509, Jgrahn, Jguk, Jiengzhen, Jh51681, Jimsve, Jizzbug, Jlin, Jnestorius, Johndci, Johnuniq, Jok2000, Jonathan Grynspan, Jonathanischoice, Jonel, Jonmon6691, Jorend, Josh Cherry, Juliano, Julienlecomte, Junkyboy55, Jyotirmay dewangan, K3rb, KJK::Hyperion, KTC, Kaimason1, Kajasudhakarababu, Kalanaki, Kapil87852007, Kashami, Kate, Keilana, Kentij, Khym Chanur, KillerGGG, KillerGurke1, Kinu, Klassobanieras, KnowledgeOfSelf, Kogz, Kooky, Korath, Koyaanis Qatsi, Krelborne, Krich, Krisnick, KristjanJonasson, Ksam, Kuru, Kusunose, Kwamikagami, Kwertii, Kxx, Kyle2^32-1, Liujiang, Lkdude, Lloyd Wood, Loadmaster, Logixoul, Lotje, Lowellian, Luks, Lvella, Lysander89, MER-C, Mabdul, Machekku, MadGeo235, Mahanga, Maheshchandrappa, Male1979, Malfuf, Malhonen, Malleus Fatuorum, Mani1, Manjo mandruva, Manofabluedog, MarSch, Marc Mongenet, Marc-André Aßbrock, Marcelo Pinto, Mark Foskey, Marktillinghast, Marqmike2, Martarius, Masterkilla, Mathrick, Mav, Maverick, Max Schwarz, Maxim, Mayank15 5, Mbecker, Mccoyst, Mcorazao, Mcstrother, Mellum, MelBanana, Mentifisto, Mephistopheltan, Metamatic, Methcub, MetsFan76, Mhnin0, MichaelJHuman, Micphi, Mifter, MihaS, Mikademus, Mike Van Emmerik, Mike92591, Mikrosam Akademija 7, MilesMi, Mindmatrix, Minesweeper, Minghong, Mipadi, Miqademus, Miranda, Mirror Vax, Mistersooreams, Mjquinn id, Mkarlesky, Mkcmkc, Mmeijeri, MoA gwang, Moanzhu, Modify, Mohamed Magdy, MoZe2386, Morwen, Moxfyre, Mpth3, Mr MaRo, Mr.GATES987, MrJeff, MrSomeone, Mrjeff, Mrwes95, Ms2ger, Muchness, Mukis, Muralive, MustafaeneS, Mxn, Myasuda, Mycplus, Mystic, N111111KKKKKKKoooooo, Naddy, Nanshu, Napi, Nasa-verve, Natdaniels, NawlinWiki, Neilc, Neurolysis, NevilleDNZ, Newsmen, Nick, Nickerr, Ninly, Nintendude, Nirvana86, Nixeagle, Njaard, Nma wiki, Nohat, Noldoaran, Non-dropframe, Noobs2007, Noosentaal, Northernhenge, ORBIT, Oddity-, Odinjobs, Ohnoitsjamie, Ojuice, OldakQuill, Oleg Alexandrov, Oliver202, Oneiros, Orderud, Ouraqt, OutRIAAge, OverlordQ, OwenBlacker, Ozzmosis, Paddu, Pak21, Pankajwillis, ParallelWolverine, Paul Stansifer, Paul evans, Paulius2003, Pavel Vozenilek, Pawanindia2009, Pbroks13, Pcb21, Pde, PeaceNT, Pedant17, Peruvianllama, Peterl, Peteturtle, Pgk, Pharaoh of the Wizards, Pharos, Phil Boswell, Philip Trueman, PhilippWeissenbacher, Pi is 3.14159, Pit, Pizza Puzzle, Plasticup, Pogipogi, Poldi, Polluxian, Polonium, Poor Yorick, Prashan08, Prohlep, ProvingReliability, Punctilius, Quadell, Quinsareth, Quuxplusone, Qwertyus, R3m0t, R4rtutorials, REggert, RN, Raghavkvp, RainbowOfLight, Ravenswood, RedBird, Redfthe, Rehabe, Reinderien, Remember the dot, Requestion, Rethorst, RexNL, Rgb1110, Rich Farmbrough, Richard Simons, Ritualizer, Rjbrock, Rjwilmsi, Roadrunner, Robdumas, Robertd, RodneyMyers, RogueMomen, Ronark, Ronhjones, Ronnyim12345, Ronyclau, Root@localhost, Rosive, Rossami, Rprpriya, Rror, Rtfb, Runus, Ruud Koot, RyanCross, Ryty01, SJP, STL, Sachin Joseph, Sadday, Sam Korn, Sango123, Sasha Slutsker, Sbisolo, Sbvb, SchfiftyThree, Schiralli, SchnitzelMannGreek, Schumi555, ScoPi, Scoops, Scorp.pankaj, Scottlemke, Scythe33, SebastianHelm, Sebastiangarth, Sebor, Sentense12, Seraphim, Sfxdude, Sg227, Shadowblade0, Shadowjams, Shawnc, SheffieldSteel, ShelfCoder, Shinjiman, Sidhantx, Sigma 7, Silsor, Simetrical, Simon G Best, SimonP, Sinternational, Sirex98, Slingada, SkyWalker, SL Sleep pilot, Sligocki, Slothy13, Smyth, Snaxe920, Sneftel, Snigbrook, Snowolf, Sohmc, SomeRandomPerson23, Sommers, Spaz man, Spiel, Spitfire, SplinterOfChaos, SpuriousQ, Stanthejeep, SteinbDJ, Stephan Schulz, Stephenb, Steve carlson, Steven Zhang, Stevenj, StewartMH, Stheller, Stoni, StradivariusTV, Strangret, Stringle, StuartYeates, Style, Suffusion of Yellow, Supertouch, Suppa chuppa, Surv1v41ist, Sutambe, SvGeloven, Svick, Swalot, Sydius, T0pem0, T4bits, TCorp, THEN WHO WAS PHONE?, Takis, TakuyaMurata, Tattema, Tbleher, TeaDrinker, Technion, Tedickey, Template namespace initialisation script, Tero, Tetra HUN, TexMurphy, The 888th Avatar, The Anome, The Inedible Bulk, The Minister of War, The Nameless, The Thing That Should Not Be, TheDeathCard, TheIncredibleEdibleOompaLoompa, TheMandarin, TheNightFly, TheSuave, TheTim, Theatrus, Thebrid, Thematrixv, Thiagomael, Thumperward, Tietew, Tifego, Tim Starling, Tim32, TingChong Ma, Tinus, Tobias Bergemann, Toffile, TomBrown16, TomCat2800, Tombrown16, Tompsci, Tony Sidaway, Torc2, Torstar.n at, Toussaint, Travroth, Trevor MacInnis, TreyHarris, Troels Arvin, Ts4z, Tslocum, Turdboy3900, Turian, Tukkkk, Umapathy, Unendra, Ungahbunga, Urod, UrsaFoot, Useight, Userabc, UtherSRG, Utnapistim, Val42, Vchimpanzee, Vincenzo.romano, Vinci0008, Viperez15, VladV, Vladimir Bosnjak, Wangi, Wavelength, Wazzup80, Werdna, Westway50, Whalelover Frost, Who, WikHead, Wikidemon, Wikidrone, Wikipendant, Wikiwonky, Willbennett2007, Wilson44691, Winchelsea, Wj32, Wknight94, Wlievens, Woohookitty, Wstaffer, Xaosflux, Xenrexisene, Xoaxdotnet, Yamla, Yankees26, Yboord028, Ybungalobill, Yoshirules367, Ysangkok, Yt95, Yurik, Zck, Zed toocool, Zenohockey, Zigmar, Zlog3, Zoe, Zr2d2, Zrs 12, Zundark, ZungBang, Zvn, Ævar Arnfjörð Bjarmason, Александр, ПешСай, Άγάμη, 无名氏, 1795 anonymous edits

SPICE Source: http://en.wikipedia.org/w/index.php?oldid=370892731 Contributors: 100110100, ACEDBA, Aandroyd, Abdull, Ademkader, Ahmednh, Akv, Altenmann, Arbustoo, Armando82, Ashokreddy2, Avian, Bassplr19, Beatnik8983, BenFrantzDale, Bmearns, Borgx, Bovineone, Brews ohare, Card, Cbdorsett, Cburnett, Chowbok, Closeapple, Daniel FR, David Haslam, Dgrant, Disavian, EffeX2, Evandobr, Ferno, Geni, Gioto, Githin, Gmoose1, Hyiu00, Ibwib, IlijaKovacevic, Jhbishop, K22rock, Kate, Kundert, Laplace99, Light current, Lisamh, Lmjohnson, Looknmall, LouScheffer, M 3bdelqader, M.e, Ma3nocum, Mako098765, Mav, MecAnt2, McSly, Michael Hardy, Minesweeper, Mythealias, Natashabaker, Ncmvocalist, Nick Pisarro, Jr., Nwk, Oasis freak england, Omegatron, PaulHanson, Pearle, Petersk, Pigsonthewing, Pion, Pjacobi, PlusMinus, Prostock123, RTC, Requestion, Rigmahroll, Rjwilmsi, Rogerbrent, Rohitbd, SMC, Scottfisher, SeanMack, Snafflekid, SpikeYoung, Stephan Leeds, Themfromspace, Tim Starling, Tom-, Tororunner, Unyoyega, Vaccardi, Visionicseda, Waveguy, Wizard191, Wladek60, Wondigoma, Wo2, Xjordanx, YoungGeezer, YukataNinja, 160 anonymous edits

C++ (programming language) *Source*: http://en.wikipedia.org/w/index.php?oldid=46023249 *Contributors*: -Barry-, 12.21.224.xxx, 223ankher, 4jobs, 4th-otaku, 7DaysForgotten, @modi, A D Monroe III, A.A.Graff, AIOS, ALOTOFTOMATOES, AMackenzie, AThing, ATren, Aandu, Abdull, Abi79, Adam12901, Addihockey10, Adi211095, Adorno rocks, Ae-a, Aesopos, Agasta, AgentFriday, Ahmadmashhour, Ahoerstemeier, Ahy1, Akeegazooka, Akersmc, Akhristov, Akihabara, Akuyume, Alan D, AlbertCahalan, AlecSchueler, Aleenf1, AlexKarpman, Alexf, Alexius08, Alexkon, Alfio, Alhoori, Aliekens, AlistairMcMillan, Allstarecho, AltiusBimm, Alxeedo, AnAccount2, AnOddName, Andante1980, Andre Engels, Andreaskem, Andrew Delong, Andrew1, AndrewHowse, AndrewKepert, Andyluciano, AngelOfSadness, Angela, Anoko moonlight, Anonymous Dissident, Antandrus, Aparna.amar.patil, Apexofservice, Arabic Pilot, Aragorn2, Arcadie, Arctic.gnome, Ardonik, Asimzb, Atjesse, Atlant, Auntof6, Austin Hair, Autopilot, Avoran, Axecution, AxelBoldt, BMW Z3, Baa, Babija, Babjisit, Bahram.zahir, Barek, Baronnet, Bart133, Bartosz, Bdragon, Belem tower, BenFrantzDale, Benhocking, Bento00, Beowulf king, Bevo, Beyondthislife, Bfzhao, Biblioth3que, Bigk105, Bill gates69, Bineet, Bkil, BlaisorBlade, Bluemoose, Bluezy, Bobazoid, Bobblewik, Bobo192, Bobthebill, Bodkinator, Boffob, Boing! said Zebedee, Bomarrow1, Bongwarrior, Booklegger, Boseko, Bovineone, Brion VIBBER, Btx40, C Labombard, C++ Template, C.Fred, CALR, CIreland, CPMcE, CRGreathouse, CWY2190, Caesura, Caiaffa, Callek, Caltas, Can't sleep, clown will eat me, CanisRufus, Cap'n Refsmmat, Capi crimm, CapitalR, Capricorn42, Captainhampton, Carabinieri, Carlson-steve, Cargt, Cathack, CecilWard, Cedars, CesarB, Cetinsert, Cfeet77, Cflm001, Cgranade, Chaos5023, CharlotteWebb, Chealer, Chocolateboy, Chrisandtaund, Christian List, Chuq, Ckburke, Cleared as filed, Closedmouth, Clsdennis2007, Cometstyles, Comperr, Conversion script, Coolwanglu, Coosbane, Coq Rouge, CordeliaNaismith, Corrector7007, Corti, Cowsnatcher27, Craig Stuntz, Crotmate, Csmaster2005, Ctu2485, Cubbi, Curps, Cwitty, Cybercobra, Cyclonenim, Cyde, Dario D., DarkHorizon, Darkmonkeyz321, Darolew, Dave Runger, Daverose 33, David A Bozzini, David H Braun (1964), Dawn Bard, Dch888, Dcoetzee, Decltype, Deibid, Delirium, Delldot, Denelson83, DerHexer, Derek Ross, Deryck Chan, DevSolar, DevastatorIC, Dibash, Diego pmc, Discospinster, Dlae, Dlfkja;lskj, Dmharvey, Dogcow, DominicConnor, DonelleDer, Donhalcon, Doofenschmirtzevilinc, DoubleRing, Doug Bell, Dougjih, Doulos Christos, Dragon, Drewcifer3000, Drrngrvy, DyInuge, Dysprosia, E Wing, ESkog, Eagleal, Earle Martin, EatMyShortz, Ebeisher, Eco84, Ecstaticfcid, Ed Brey, Edward Z. Yang, Eelis, Eelis.net, Ehn, Elliskev, Elysdir, Enarsee, EncMstr, Enerjazzer, EngineerScotty, Eric119, ErikHaugen, Esanchez7587, Esben, Esmito, Esrogs, Eternaldescent08, Ethan, EvanED, Evice, Evil Monkey, Ewok18, Excirial, FW4NK, Fa2sA, Facorread, Faithlessthewonderboy, Faizni, Falcon300000, Fanf, Fashionslide, FatalError, Favonian, Fistboy, Fizzackerly, Flaminganticchimp, Flash200, Flewis, Flex, Flyingprogrammer, FrancoGG, Freakofnurture, Frecklefoot, Free Software Knight, Freshneeesz, Fritzpoll, Fubhrygyn, Furby100, Furrykef, Fuzzybyte, GLari, Gaul, Gauss, Geeoharee, Gene.thomas, Gengiskanhg, Giftlite, Gil mo, Gildos, Gilgamesh, Gilliam, Gimili2, Gimme danger, Gmcfoley, God Of All, Gogo Dodo, GoodSirJava, Graue, Greatdebtor, GregorB, Gremagor, Grenavitar, Grey GosHawk, Grigor The Ox, Gsonnenf, Gusmoe, Gwern, Gwjames, Hairy Dude, Hakkinen, HappyCamper, Harald Hansen, Harinisanthosh, Harryboyles, HebrewHammerTime, HeikoEvermann, Hemanshu, HenryLi, Herorev, Hervegirod, Hetar, Hgfernan, HideandLeek, Hihahiha474, Hiraku.n, Hmains, Hobartimus, Hogman500, Horselover Frost, Hoss7994, Hu, Hu12, Husond, Hyad, Hyperfusion, I already forgot, ISoLoveHer, Iamninja91, Ibroadfo, Imc, Immunize, InShanece, Innocent, Insanity Incarnate, Intangir, Iphoneorange, Iridescence, Iridescent, Irish Souffle, Ironholds, Isaacl, Ixfd64, J Casanova, J Di, J-A-V-A, J.delanoy, JForget, JNighthawk, Jackelfive, Jafet, Jarednf, Jatos, Javiercastillo73, Javierito92, Jawed, Jayaram ganapathy, Jdent29, Jdowland, Jeff G, JeffTL, Jeltz, Jerry teps, Jerryobject, Jeshan, Jesse Viviano, JesseW, Jgamer509, Jgrahn, Jgroenen, Jh51681, Jimsve, Jizzbug, Jlin, Jnestorius, Johndci, Johnniq, Jok2000, Jonathan Grynspan, Jonathanischoice, Jonel, Jonmon6691, Jorend, Josh Cherry, Juliano, Julienlecomte, Junkyboy55, Jyotirmay dewangan, K3rb, KJK::Hyperion, KTC, Kaimason1, Kajasudhakarababu, Kalanaki, Kapil87852007, Kashami, Kate, Keilana, Kentij, Khym Chanur, Kifcaliph, King of Hearts, Kinu, Klassohanieras, KnowledgeOfSelf, Kogz, Kooky, Korath, Koyaanis Qatsi, Krelborne, Krich, Krischik, Kristjan.Jonasson, Ksam, Kuru, Kusunose, Kwamikagami, Kwertii, Kxx, Kyle2*32-1, Kyleahampton, Landon1980, Larry V, Lars Washington, Lastplacer, Le Funtime Frankie, Lee Daniel Crocker, LeinadSpoon, Liao, Liftarn, Lightmouse, Ligulem, Lilac Soul, Lilpony6225, Lir, Liujiang, Lkdude, Lloyd Wood, Loadmaster, Logixoul, Lotje, Lowellian, Luks, Lvella, Lysander89, MER-C, Mabdul, Machekku, MadCow257, Mahanga, Maheshchowdary, Male1979, Malfuf, Malhonen, Malleus Fatuorum, Mani1, Manjo mandruva, Manofabluedog, MarSch, Marc Mongenet, Marc-André ABbrock, Marcelo Pinto, Mark Foskey, Marktillinghast, Marqmike2, Martarius, Masterkilla, Mathrick, Mav, Mavarok, Max Schwarz, Maxim, MayankI5 5, Mbecker, Mccoyst, Mcorazao, Mcstrother, Mellum, MeltBanana, Mentifisto, Mephistophelian, Metamatic, Methcub, MetsFan76, Mhnin0, MichaelJHuman, Micphi, Mifter, MihaS, Mikademus, Mike Van Emmerik, Mike92591, Mikrosam Akademija 7, MilesMi, Mindmatrix, Minesweeper, Minghong, Mipadi, Miqademus, Miranda, Mirror Vax, Mistersooreams, Mjquinn id, Mkarlesky, Mkcmkc, Mmeijeri, MoAIgnome, Moanzhu, Modify, Mohamed Magdy, Mole2386, Morwen, Moxfyre, Mptb3, Mr MaRo, Mr.GATES987, MrJeff, MrSomeone, Mrjeff, Mrwes95, Ms2ger, Muchness, Mukis, Muralive, Mustafaene5, Mxn, Myasuda, Myceplus, Mystic, N111111KKKKKKKooooo, Naddy, Nanshu, Napi, Nasa-verve, Natdaniels, NawlinWiki, Neilc, Neurolysis, NevilleDNZ, Newsmen, Nick, Nicsterr, Ninly, Nintendude, Nirdh, Nisheet88, Nixeagle, Njuard, Nma wiki, Nohat, Noldoaran, Non-dropframe, Noobs2007, Noosentaal, Northernhenge, ORBIT, Oddity-, Odinjobs, Ohnoitsjamie, Ojuice, OldakQuill, Oleg Alexandrov, Oliver202, Oneiros, Orderud, Ouraqt, OutRIAAge, OverlordQ, OwenBlacker, Ozzmosis, Paddu, Pak21, Pankajwillis, ParallelWolverine, Paul Stansifer, Paul evans, Paulius2003, Pavel Vozenilek, Pawanindia2009, Pbroks13, Pcb21, Pde, PeaceNT, Pedant17, PeruvianIlama, Peterl, Peteturtle, Pgk, Pharaoh of the Wizards, Pharos, Phil Boswell, Philip Trueman, PhilippWeissenbacher, Pi is 3.14159, Pit, Pizza Puzzle, Plasticup, Pogipogi, Poldi, Polluxian, Polonium, Poor Yorick, Prashan08, Prohlep, ProvingReliabilty, Punctilius, Quadell, Quinsareth, Quuxplusone, Qwertyus, R3mOt, R4rtutorials, REggert, RN, Raghavkvp, RainbowOfLight, Ravisankarvn, Rbonvall, Rdsmith4, RedWolf, Rehabe, Reinderien, Remember the dot, Requestion, Rethnor, RexNL, Rgb1110, Rich Farmbrough, Richard Simons, Ritualizer, Rjbrock, Rjwilmsi, Roadrunner, Robdumas, Robertd, RodneyMyers, RogueMomen, Ronark, Ronhjones, Ronnyim12345, Ronyclau, Root@localhost, Rosive, Rossami, Rprpriya, Rror, Rtfb, Rursus, Ruud Koot, RyanCross, Ryty01, SJP, STL, Sachin Joseph, Sadday, Saimhe, Samuel, Sandahl, Sasha Slutsker, Sbisolo, Sbvb, SchfiftyThree, Schiralli, SchnitzelMannGreek, Schumi555, ScoPi, Scoops, Scorp.pankaj, Scottlemke, Scythe33, SebastianHelm, Sebastiangarth, Sebor, Sentense12, Seraphim, Sfxdude, Sg227, Shadowblade0, Shadowjams, Shawne, SheffieldSteel, ShellCoder, Shinjiman, Sidhantx, Sigma 7, Silsor, Simetrical, Simon G Best, SimonP, Sinternational, Sirex98, Sishgupta, Sittethief, Skew-t, Skizzik, SkyWalker, SI, Sleep pilot, Sligocki, Slothy13, Smyth, Snaxe920, Sneftel, Snigbrook, Snowolf, Sohmc, SomeRandomPerson23, Sommers, Spaz man, Spiel, Spitfire, SplinterOfChaos, SpuriousQ, Stanthejeep, SteinbDJ, Stephan Schulz, Stephenb, Steve carlson, Steven Zhang, Stevenj, StewartMH, Stheller, Stoni, StoptheDatabaseState, Strangnet, Stringle, Stuartclift, Style, Suffusion of Yellow, Supertouch, Suppa chuppa, Surv1v4l1st, Sutambe, SvGeloven, Svick, Swalot, Sydius, T0pem0, T4bits, TCorp, THEN WHO WAS PHONE?, Takis, TakuyaMurata, Tattema, Tbleher, TeaDrinker, Technion, Tedickey, Template namespace initialisation script, Tero, Tetra HUN, TexMurphy, The 888th Avatar, The Anome, The Inedible Bulk, The Minister of War, The Nameless, The Thing That Should Not Be, TheDeathCard, TheIncredibleEdibleOompaLoompa, TheMandarin, TheNightFly, TheSuave, TheTim, Theatrus, Thebrid, Thematrixv, Thiagomael, Thumperward, Tietew, Tifego, Tim Starling, Tim32, TingChong Ma, Tinus, Tobias Bergemann, Toffile, TomBrown16, TomCat2800, Tombrown16, Tompsci, Tony Sidaway, Torc2, Tordek ar, Toussaint, Traroth, Trevor MacInnis, TreyHarris, Troels Arvin, Ts4z, Tslocum, Turdbgo3900, Turian, TuukkaH, Ubardak, Umapathy, Unendra, Urod, UrsaFoot, Useight, Userabc, UtherSRG, Utnapistim, Val42, Vchimpanzee, Vincenzo.romano, Vinci0008, Viperez15, VladV, Vladimir Bosnjak, Wangi, Wavelength, Wazzup80, Werdna, Westway50, Whaleiover Frost, Who, WikHead, Wikidemon, Wikidrone, Winston365, WillBennett2007, Wilson44691, Winchelsea, Wj32, Wknight94, Wlievens, Woohookitty, Wsikard, XJamRastafire, Xerxesnine, Xoaxdotnet, Yamla, Yankees26, Yboord028, Ybungalobill, Yoshirules367, Ysangkok, Yt95, Yurik, Zck, Zed toocool, Zenohockey, Zigmar, Zlog3, Zoe, Zr2d2, Zrs 12, Zundark, ZungBang, Zvn, Ævar Arnfjörð Bjarmason, Александр, ПешСай, Аγύπη, 无名氏, 1795 anonymous edits

Electronic design automation *Source*: http://en.wikipedia.org/w/index.php?oldid=366487703 *Contributors*: Aditya shiledar, Af648, Agasta, Agrawalyogesh04, Alphachimp, Altenmann, Arioshahbani, Astaroth5, Bigfool, Bing11, Bovineone, Brengi, Brorson, Bruce89, Ccolin2509, Cheese Sandwich, Chounder, Chris the speller, Cjdavis, Cosmic Engine, Dhishnawiki, Dicklyon, Doreecchio, Droll, Duk, Edward Z. Yang, Ekotkie, ElderDelp, Electron9, EncMstr, Engineer Bob, Euoa, Evercat, Foobarhoge, Frap, Galoubet, Geni, Gmoose1, Gnaeme1., Gurch, Harvester, Hjamleh, Hu12, HumphreyW, Jcarroll, Jeff3000, Jni, Jovianeye, Jpbowen, KaiMartin, Kglavin, King4057, Kozuch, Krishnavedala, LLanders, Lamkin, Leon7, LiberalFascist, Light current, Lighthievesall, LouScheffer, Macallan25, Madhubanti, Mboverload, Mdd4696, Mg886112, Mic, Michael Hardy, Microsp, Momoricks, Mrand, MySchizoBuddy, NSR, Naohiro19 revertvandal, Nixdorf, Panscient, Parikshit Narkhede, Patrickyip, Philewar, Pigsonthewing, PlusMinus, Poppafuze, RedWolf, ReeH, Requestion, Ronz, Rrburke, Saxifrage, Scootey, Scottfisher, Sephiroth BCR, Shahimbaker, Softogo, Sramana18, Startup101, Steven Hepting, Strubin, Suruena, Sylvain Mielot, Taylorhogan, TeamX, Thewocost, Tomjenkins52, Typeriuskirk, Verilog, Vish.ak, Welsh, Wik, WimdeValk, Winwiz88, Woz2, Youssefa, Yurivict, Zzuuzz, 200 anonymous edits

Biquad filter *Source*: http://en.wikipedia.org/w/index.php?oldid=354385466 *Contributors*: Alvin Seville, C J Cowie, Harej, Inductiveload, PAR, Sandstein, SoftwareLibre, Spinningspark, TedPavlic, Torc2, TwinsMetsFan, 6 anonymous edits

Complex frequency *Source*: http://en.wikipedia.org/w/index.php?oldid=260532187 *Contributors*: BD2412, BenFrantzDale, Can't sleep, clown will eat me, Centrx, Charles Matthews, Chetvorno, Derek56, DragonflySixtyseven, Foobaz, INVERTED, Mcleodm, RekishiEJ, Robin48gx, Yardleydohon, 8 anonymous edits

Circuit analysis *Source*: http://en.wikipedia.org/w/index.php?oldid=203791913 *Contributors*: Abdull, Alberto Orlandini, Alfred Centauri, Ali@gwc.org.uk, Beniek, BillC, Bpeps, Cbdorsett, Charles Matthews, Colinpan, Crl620, Dan Granahan, Dbenbenn, DerHexer, Doctorfluffy, E Wing, Enok.cc, Gaius Cornelius, Greggwon, Heron, Hpmemproject, Jurgen Hissen, Katieh5584, Koavf, Lil chef1, Mamling, Michael Hardy, Mild Bill Hiccup, Mlewis000, Mrball25, Mythealias, Nabla, Omegatron, PP Jewel, Pakaraki, Plugwash, Prara, RDBrown, RJFJR, Rjwilmsi, Rogerbrent, Rogger.Ferguson, Sergeroz, Shyam, SimonP, Spinningspark, The Photon, Themfromspace, TomyDuby, Tsi43318, Undsoweiter, Yazaq, 64 anonymous edits

Analytical expression *Source*: http://en.wikipedia.org/w/index.php?oldid=331986828 *Contributors*: DS1000, Gtdj, Lambiam, Mathsci, 3 anonymous edits

Image Sources, Licenses and Contributors

File:Windows logo.svg *Source*: http://en.wikipedia.org/w/index.php?title=File:Windows_logo.svg *License*: unknown *Contributors*: Blubberboy92, Cflm001, FleetCommand, Koman90, Tyw7, Zzyzx11, 3 anonymous edits

File:Windows 7.png *Source*: http://en.wikipedia.org/w/index.php?title=File:Windows_7.png *License*: unknown *Contributors*: Addihockey10, Althepal, AnOddName, Anakin101, Andyso, AussieLegend, Crazlunatic, Drilnoth, Feinoha, GSK, Grayshi, James Michael 1, Jan Hofmann, Jjupiter100, Josh the Nerd, LOL, LobStoR, Mephiles602, Ngyikp, OriginalGamer, PhilKnight, RegularBreaker, S0aasdf2sf, SF007, SchuminWeb, Sdrtirs, Sonicdude558, Sotcr, SpaceFlight89, The 888th Avatar, Warren, Wtshymanski, 27 anonymous edits

File:Windows1.0.png *Source*: http://en.wikipedia.org/w/index.php?title=File:Windows1.0.png *License*: unknown *Contributors*: Aiyizo, Diego Moya, Frogger3140, Gan Luo, Ghettoblaster, Happy Dude, James Michael 1, Kubek15, Michaelkourlas, Neurolysis, Remember the dot, Warren, 3 anonymous edits

File:Windows 3.0 workspace.png *Source*: http://en.wikipedia.org/w/index.php?title=File:Windows_3.0_workspace.png *License*: unknown *Contributors*: Dancraggs, James Michael 1, Shlomital, Tyomitch, Warren, Yamla, 4 anonymous edits

File:Am windows95 desktop.png *Source*: http://en.wikipedia.org/w/index.php?title=File:Am_windows95_desktop.png *License*: unknown *Contributors*: AlistairMcMillan, Damian Yerrick, Diego Moya, Ghettoblaster, James Michael 1, Koman90, McLoaf, Shlomital, ViperSnake151, Warren, 4 anonymous edits

File:WindowsCE7.jpg *Source*: http://en.wikipedia.org/w/index.php?title=File:WindowsCE7.jpg *License*: unknown *Contributors*: Interframe

Image:Windows Family Tree.svg *Source*: http://en.wikipedia.org/w/index.php?title=File:Windows_Family_Tree.svg *License*: Creative Commons Attribution 2.5 *Contributors*: J.int, Linfocito B, NOKIA 3120 classic, 1 anonymous edits

Image:Orcad schematic capture.PNG *Source*: http://en.wikipedia.org/w/index.php?title=File:Orcad_schematic_capture.PNG *License*: unknown *Contributors*: Basilicofresco, ESkog, Kglavin, Omegatron, 2 anonymous edits

Image:Gschem.png *Source*: http://en.wikipedia.org/w/index.php?title=File:Gschem.png *License*: unknown *Contributors*: User:Omegatron

Image:Biquad circuit.gif *Source*: http://en.wikipedia.org/w/index.php?title=File:Biquad_circuit.gif *License*: Public Domain *Contributors*: Ben Rodanski

Image:Pierre-Simon Laplace.jpg *Source*: http://en.wikipedia.org/w/index.php?title=File:Pierre-Simon_Laplace.jpg *License*: unknown *Contributors*: Ashill, Elcobbola, Gene.arboit, Jimmy44, Olivier2, 蕃木瓜二

Image:Rotating spherical harmonics.gif *Source*: http://en.wikipedia.org/w/index.php?title=File:Rotating_spherical_harmonics.gif *License*: GNU Free Documentation License *Contributors*: Cyp, Jengelh, Pieter Kuiper, 1 anonymous edits

Image:Laplace house Arcueil.jpg *Source*: http://en.wikipedia.org/w/index.php?title=File:Laplace_house_Arcueil.jpg *License*: unknown *Contributors*: User:cutler

Image:Pierre-Simon-Laplace (1749-1827).jpg *Source*: http://en.wikipedia.org/w/index.php?title=File:Pierre-Simon-Laplace_(1749-1827).jpg *License*: unknown *Contributors*: Gabor, Luestling, Olivier2, Umherirrender

Image:C plus plus book.jpg *Source*: http://en.wikipedia.org/w/index.php?title=File:C_plus_plus_book.jpg *License*: unknown *Contributors*: Cybercobra, ICReal, Jusjih, Michaelas10, NAHID, Skier Dude, Storkk, Suffusion of Yellow, Yamla, 5 anonymous edits

File:Wikibooks-logo-en.svg *Source*: http://en.wikipedia.org/w/index.php?title=File:Wikibooks-logo-en.svg *License*: logo *Contributors*: User:Bastique, User:Ramac

Image:BjarneStroustrup.jpg *Source*: http://en.wikipedia.org/w/index.php?title=File:BjarneStroustrup.jpg *License*: GNU Free Documentation License *Contributors*: -

Image:Kicad Pcbnew screenshot.jpg *Source*: http://en.wikipedia.org/w/index.php?title=File:Kicad_Pcbnew_screenshot.jpg *License*: GNU General Public License *Contributors*: Bitsrc, Ö, 1 anonymous edits

Image:Kicad Pcbnew3D screenshot.jpg *Source*: http://en.wikipedia.org/w/index.php?title=File:Kicad_Pcbnew3D_screenshot.jpg *License*: GNU General Public License *Contributors*: Bitsrc, Ö

Image:Kicad Eeschema screenshot.jpg *Source*: http://en.wikipedia.org/w/index.php?title=File:Kicad_Eeschema_screenshot.jpg *License*: GNU General Public License *Contributors*: Athaenara, Bitsrc, Ö

Image:Gschem and gerbv.jpg *Source*: http://en.wikipedia.org/w/index.php?title=File:Gschem_and_gerbv.jpg *License*: Creative Commons Attribution 3.0 *Contributors*: Peter Clifton

Image:Image Filter L Half-section.svg *Source*: http://en.wikipedia.org/w/index.php?title=File:Image_Filter_L,_Half-section.svg *License*: Public Domain *Contributors*: User:Inductiveload

Image:Image filter T Section.svg *Source*: http://en.wikipedia.org/w/index.php?title=File:Image_filter_T_Section.svg *License*: Public Domain *Contributors*: User:Inductiveload

Image:Image filter PI Section.svg *Source*: http://en.wikipedia.org/w/index.php?title=File:Image_filter_Pi_Section.svg *License*: Public Domain *Contributors*: User:Inductiveload

Image:Image Filter Ladder Network (Unbalanced).svg *Source*: http://en.wikipedia.org/w/index.php?title=File:Image_Filter_Ladder_Network_(Unbalanced).svg *License*: Public Domain *Contributors*: User:Inductiveload

Image:Image Filter C Half-section.svg *Source*: http://en.wikipedia.org/w/index.php?title=File:Image_Filter_C_Half-section.svg *License*: Public Domain *Contributors*: User:Inductiveload

Image:Image Filter H Section.svg *Source*: http://en.wikipedia.org/w/index.php?title=File:Image_Filter_H_Section.svg *License*: Public Domain *Contributors*: User:Inductiveload

Image:Image Filter Box Section.svg *Source*: http://en.wikipedia.org/w/index.php?title=File:Image_Filter_Box_Section.svg *License*: Public Domain *Contributors*: User:Inductiveload

Image:Image Filter Ladder Network (Balanced).svg *Source*: http://en.wikipedia.org/w/index.php?title=File:Image_Filter_Ladder_Network_(Balanced).svg *License*: Public Domain *Contributors*: User:Inductiveload

Image:Image Filter X Section.svg *Source*: http://en.wikipedia.org/w/index.php?title=File:Image_filter_X_Section.svg *License*: Public Domain *Contributors*: User:Inductiveload

Image:Image filter X Section (Pi-Derived).svg *Source*: http://en.wikipedia.org/w/index.php?title=File:Image_filter_X_Section_(Pi-Derived).svg *License*: Public Domain *Contributors*: User:Inductiveload

File:M-Derived Series Filter Half-section.svg *Source*: http://en.wikipedia.org/w/index.php?title=File:M-Derived_Series_Filter_Half-section.svg *License*: Public Domain *Contributors*: User:Inductiveload

File:Zobel Bridged-T Filter.svg *Source*: http://en.wikipedia.org/w/index.php?title=File:Zobel_Bridged-T_Filter.svg *License*: Creative Commons Attribution-Sharealike 3.0 *Contributors*: User:Inductiveload

File:Lattice All-pass Phase Correction Filter.svg *Source*: http://en.wikipedia.org/w/index.php?title=File:Lattice_All-pass_Phase_Correction_Filter.svg *License*: Public Domain *Contributors*: User:Inductiveload

Image:MFB Topology.png *Source*: http://en.wikipedia.org/w/index.php?title=File:MFB_Topology.png *License*: Public Domain *Contributors*: User:PAR

Image:BiquadFilter1.PNG *Source*: http://en.wikipedia.org/w/index.php?title=File:BiquadFilter1.PNG *License*: Creative Commons Attribution-Sharealike 2.5 *Contributors*: Ironphoenix

File:Resistor button.svg *Source*: http://en.wikipedia.org/w/index.php?title=File:Resistor_button.svg *License*: Creative Commons Attribution-Sharealike 3.0 *Contributors*: User:Spinningspark

File:Capacitor button.svg *Source*: http://en.wikipedia.org/w/index.php?title=File:Capacitor_button.svg *License*: Creative Commons Attribution-Sharealike 3.0 *Contributors*: User:Spinningspark

File:Inductor button.svg *Source*: http://en.wikipedia.org/w/index.php?title=File:Inductor_button.svg *License*: Creative Commons Attribution-Sharealike 3.0 *Contributors*: User:Spinningspark

File:Reactance button.svg *Source*: http://en.wikipedia.org/w/index.php?title=File:Reactance_button.svg *License*: Creative Commons Attribution-Sharealike 3.0 *Contributors*: User:Spinningspark

File:Impedance button.svg *Source*: http://en.wikipedia.org/w/index.php?title=File:Impedance_button.svg *License*: Creative Commons Attribution-Sharealike 3.0 *Contributors*: User:Spinningspark

File:Voltage button.svg *Source*: http://en.wikipedia.org/w/index.php?title=File:Voltage_button.svg *License*: Creative Commons Attribution-Sharealike 3.0 *Contributors*: User:Spinningspark

File:Conductance button.svg *Source*: http://en.wikipedia.org/w/index.php?title=File:Conductance_button.svg *License*: Creative Commons Attribution-Sharealike 3.0 *Contributors*: User:Spinningspark

File:Elastance button.svg *Source*: http://en.wikipedia.org/w/index.php?title=File:Elastance_button.svg *License*: Creative Commons Attribution-Sharealike 3.0 *Contributors*: User:Spinningspark

File:Blank button.svg *Source*: http://en.wikipedia.org/w/index.php?title=File:Blank_button.svg *License*: Creative Commons Attribution-Sharealike 3.0 *Contributors*: User:Spinningspark

File:Susceptance button.svg *Source*: http://en.wikipedia.org/w/index.php?title=File:Susceptance_button.svg *License*: Creative Commons Attribution-Sharealike 3.0 *Contributors*: User:Spinningspark

License

Lightning Source UK Ltd.
Milton Keynes UK
UKOW051017140112